THE ART OF THE NEW YORKER
1925~1995

THE ART OF
THE NEW YORKER
1925~1995

LEE LORENZ

ALFRED A. KNOPF   NEW YORK

1995

THIS IS A BORZOI BOOK
PUBLISHED BY ALFRED A. KNOPF, INC.

Library of Congress Cataloging-in-Publication Data

Lorenz, Lee.
    The art of the New Yorker, 1925–1995 / Lee Lorenz.—1st ed.
        p.   cm.
    ISBN 0-679-43679-0
    1. Caricatures and cartoons—United States.   2. American wit and humor, Pictorial.
I. Title.
NC1428.N47   1995
741.6´52´0973—dc20   95-5249
                                                                       CIP

Manufactured in the United States of America
First Edition

This book is dedicated to the artists
of *The New Yorker*—past, present, and future.

INDUSTRIAL CRISIS

The day a cake of Ivory sank at Proctor & Gamble's

INTRODUCTION

The Art of The New Yorker began more than fifty years ago on the sunporch of my grandparents' home in Wood-Ridge, New Jersey. The bookshelves that ran beneath the windows were filled with copies of The New Yorker, and the long, tranquil hours I spent leafing through their pages are among the happiest memories of my childhood. The captions under the cartoons meant nothing to me, but the drawings themselves had a variety and richness I found irresistible.

The magazine had been introduced to the household by my mother, then a college student fired with literary ambitions. She and her small circle of like-minded friends gathered weekly to share the smart new journal that, for them, epitomized the clever and sophisticated world that sparkled so seductively on the other side of the Hudson. Although my mother's literary aspirations were never fulfilled, The New Yorker continued to be a valued presence in our household and, later, a weekly tonic during my first lonely years away at college.

At that point The New Yorker had become for me, as it has for many readers, much more than a magazine. Its weekly arrival invoked the fabled world of Ross, White, Thurber, and the Algonquin Round Table. Piecing together the history of the magazine's art, I have discovered a story that combines improbable characters and an implausible plot in a manner as unexpected and satisfying as any fable. This story has the added charm of being true.

Since its birth in 1925, The New Yorker has published thousands of pieces of art produced by hundreds of artists. This great mountain of material rests on a foundation of notes, letters, and, most importantly, memos, now carefully filed in The New Yorker archives at the New York Public Library. The abundance and quality of this material are both astounding and daunting. The memos are not the expected two-line zingers, but long, typewritten, occasionally impassioned communications often running to several pages. In 1943, for example, Ross produced over an eight-day period three bristling communiqués to the accounting department, which dealt solely with the question of whether or not Saul Steinberg had received a small overpayment for two spot drawings.

There are treasures here to delight students of popular journalism, social critics, art historians, and analysts of twentieth-century American humor. A substantial book on *The New Yorker* art could be produced from any of these perspectives. My reading of this material is, of course, through the lens of my thirty-five years at the magazine: first as a cartoonist and later as art editor.

All this is to say that, inside this modest two-hundred-page book (less than three pages for each year of the magazine's life), a much fatter volume is crying to get out. My hope is that this initial effort will provide a useful armature for more comprehensive work to come.

This year, *The New Yorker* is celebrating its seventieth birthday. To have reached such a Methuselean age in the turbulent world of contemporary publishing is remarkable. To move into one's eighth decade with the energy and enthusiasm that characterize today's magazine is extraordinary. Much of this energy flows from the magazine's artists—a blend of seasoned contributors and fresh new voices that now stretches from Arno to Avedon.

From the magazine's anxious early years to the confident present, the artists have provided the music to which the magazine marches. Their exuberance and resourcefulness show no signs of flagging, and promise unimagined delights in the decades ahead.

THE ART OF THE NEW YORKER
1925~1995

I T   A L L   B E G I N S with Ross.

He was born Harold Wallace Ross in Aspen, Colorado, in 1892. Shortly afterward his parents moved to Salt Lake City. The contradictions that defined Ross spring from his parentage. His father was a miner, sharp-tongued, quick-witted, and disputatious. (The one thing he seemed to enjoy about Salt Lake City was baiting his Mormon neighbors over obscure points of scripture.) His mother was quiet, practical-minded, and an earnest Scot-Presbyterian. Ross appears to have inherited his roustabout's vocabulary and his sardonic wit from one and his Victorian prudishness and his staying power from the other.

Like many adolescents, Ross read and dreamed of adventure. His favorite writers were Jack London and Joseph Conrad. The Russo-Japanese War was headline news, and, seeking to escape from an overbearing father and indulge his taste for adventure, he fantasized about becoming a war correspondent. He took to hanging around the local paper, where a high school chum, John Held, Jr., was already working as a cartoonist. At the end of his sophomore year he dropped out of school to become an itinerant newspaperman. The proliferation of newspapers at the turn of the century had created a steady demand for competent rewrite men and reporters. In response to this, a new breed of freelance journalists appeared. They were a hard-drinking, tough-talking, and fiercely independent bunch. When Ross joined their ranks he felt, possibly for the first time in his life, at home.

Though most of Ross's colleagues on the road were self-educated men, they were widely read, and his own education seems to have been completed by long, occasionally drunken conversations about politics, religion, and, of course, literature. While working his way back and forth across the country, Ross added to his list of favorite authors. He read and responded to the philosopher and social critic Herbert Spencer. He was particularly drawn to Mark Twain. Twain's observations on style, as recorded in "Fenimore Cooper's Literary Offenses," seem to have provided the model for Ross's later career as an editor. Twain came down hard on Cooper over questions of plausibility, and Ross was fanatical about getting the facts straight. Twain also called for "a simple and straightforward style" in which the author should *say* what he is proposing to say, not merely come near it." Saul Steinberg once said to me, "Ah, Ross, I give you a hint. Huckleberry Finn."

Ross supplemented his spotty wages as a reporter with his winnings at cribbage, which were often substantial, and at poker, which were often in-

Ross, his hair uncharacteristically flat, in an early studio shot

Opposite:
Rea Irvin's sketch for *The New Yorker*'s first cover. The bar running down the left side seems to have been Ross's idea. It was meant to suggest the spine of a book, and allowed the magazine to adjust its proportions (as it has over the years) without cropping the art.

consequential. His taste for high-stakes gambling occasionally put him next to people from more rarefied educational and professional backgrounds. These brushes with the gentry did nothing to smooth Ross's rough edges, but they did increase his already substantial self-confidence.

In the spring of 1917 Ross impulsively enlisted in the army and was shipped abroad. While stationed in Bordeaux, he discovered that a paper for the servicemen was being organized in Paris and he promptly went AWOL to join it.

As one of the first members of the *Stars and Stripes* staff, Ross became a member of its informal editorial "board." The editor was an intense, humorless zealot named Guy T. Viskniskki, and when the staff eased him out in a bloodless coup, Ross, seemingly by default, took over. It was his first editorial experience. He learned how to lay out a page and how to edit copy. He learned how to bring order out of the chaos of the newsroom. Ross the hobo-journalist became Ross the martinet editor. *The Stars and Stripes* put Ross in touch with well-established talents, including Grantland Rice, the sports columnist, Heywood Broun from *Judge* magazine, and Franklin P. Adams, whose widely read column in the New York *Tribune*, "The Conning Tower," was an important showcase for smart young writers and poets.

In terms of Ross's future, his most important association was with a pudgy and remarkably pugnacious young journalist named Alexander Woollcott. Woollcott already had a substantial reputation as a writer and critic, and though he and Ross came from quite different backgrounds, they shared a taste for vituperative repartee, poker, and cribbage. Woollcott was a man who collected people, and Ross was eminently collectible. Shaping lives was a habit, perhaps a vice, of Woollcott's, and in later years he attempted to take up E. B. White in the same manner. (White, however, proved immune to the fabled Woollcott charm. He later described Woollcott as "an old poop.")

The staff gathered nightly at a local bistro called Nini's, and it was at these regular poker sessions, which later evolved into the Thanatopsis Literary and Inside Straight Club, that Ross began musing aloud about starting an upscale weekly tabloid. Initially, he seems to have been inspired as much by a sentimental desire to keep the *Stars and Stripes* crowd together as by any clear literary ambition. Woollcott listened encouragingly. He had already confided to a few friends that he thought Ross had a special, quirky gift that could find an outlet only in the publishing world of Manhattan. He even enlisted an old flame, Jane Grant, who was also in Paris, in his

The young Ross, with mane rising

campaign to bring Ross back to New York. Woollcott was so successful at this that a romance developed between Ross and Grant.

As the war wound down, Ross discovered yet another aspect of his personality, a latent entrepreneurial instinct. He and a few pals published a collection of jokes which had been submitted by soldiers to *The Stars and Stripes*. They financed the venture out of their own pockets and sold them back to the soldiers under the title *Yank Talk*. This cut-and-paste enterprise was an unexpected success. The Red Cross bought fifty thousand copies to distribute to the troops, and Ross quickly brought out a sequel, *More Yank Talk*. The easy success of this venture, which, like Franklin P. Adams's "Conning Tower," was fueled entirely by unsolicited and unpaid-for work, may have some bearing on Ross's later, unrealistic expectations for filling the pages of his own magazine.

When the war ended and the *Stars and Stripes* crew began preparing to reenter civilian life, Woollcott stepped up his campaign to lure Ross to New York. Ross was torn. He had attempted to get a job in New York before the war and he never got any closer than Hoboken. He talked vaguely about taking his nest egg and loafing in the South Seas. At the same time, he was deeply involved with Jane Grant, who was returning to her job in Manhattan at *The New York Times*. The persuasive powers of Woollcott notwithstanding, Ross's decision was finally made on the basis of a job offer from an unlikely source. A large publisher, Butterick, was floating the idea of a successor to *The Stars and Stripes*, *The Home Sector*, to be published in the States after the war. Ross and his companions were invited to become the editorial board. Ross agreed to sign on as editor. Other *Stars and Stripes* staffers followed. These included Woollcott, George Boas, the cartoonist Wally Wallgren, and Tyler Bliss, who later became Ross's first managing editor at *The New Yorker*. Salaries were generous—Ross got a hundred dollars a week—and the prospects seemed encouraging. However, poor management and a crippling printers' strike did in the magazine early. It published its last issue on April 17, 1920.

Almost immediately, Ross and his friends were offered another position at a new and already flourishing magazine published by the American Legion called, simply, *American Legion Weekly*. Again, the salary was good, and again Ross assumed the position of editor. By this time Ross was feeling at home in New York. He was established in a "ménage à quatre" with Jane Grant (now his wife), Heywood Broun, and Broun's wife, Ruth Hale. Alexander Woollcott had introduced Ross to the Algonquin circle, where they reestablished the Thanatopsis Literary and Inside Straight Club. The

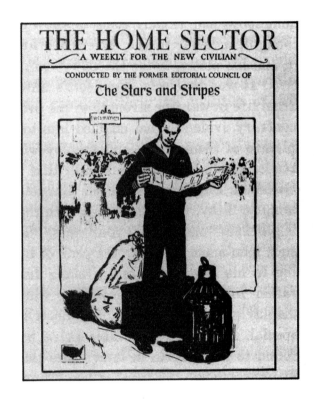

Ross and Jane Grant at their first Manhattan digs

Algonquin bunch included, in addition to Woollcott, Franklin P. Adams, Robert Benchley, George S. Kaufman, Marc Connelly, Edna Ferber, and Dorothy Parker. Ross more than held his own with this quick-witted group, but for once he listened more than he talked. The ease with which his companions tossed off one-liners must have convinced Ross that the streets of Manhattan were indeed paved with gold.

Ross was increasingly restless at *American Legion*. It was essentially a house organ. There was little opportunity for him to experiment or hire new talent, but with no other prospects in sight, he hung on. Then, in 1924, he received an unexpected offer. The printer of *American Legion* purchased a controlling interest in the humor magazine *Judge* and invited Ross to become coeditor. Ross saw this as a chance to put into practice some of the ideas he and Jane Grant had been developing for a humor weekly. In fact, Ross's stint at *Judge* was short and dispiriting. The magazine was slipping when he joined it, and his efforts did nothing to slow its decline. Readers were being offered five dollars a shot to send in "Krazy Kracks." A typical regular feature was one called "Funnybones," short gags printed inside balloons shaped like a dog's bone. Ross quit after only a few months and began working in earnest on his proposal for a sophisticated metropolitan weekly. By this time he had a pretty good idea of what his magazine would offer.

Ross estimated, incorrectly as it turned out, that he could float his project for fifty thousand dollars. Between them, he and Jane Grant had twenty-five. Working his way through his better-heeled gambling pals, Ross eventually targeted the scion of a prosperous bakery businessman, Raoul Fleischmann. (Fleischmann's yeast company was controlled by other members of the same family.) Ross's first approach to Fleischmann was not a success. In fact, if Ross had been a better salesman, *The New Yorker* might never have been born. Forced at their first meeting to put his proposal down in black and white, Ross got cold feet, and, according to Jane Grant, he suggested to Fleischmann that he back an earlier idea of Ross's for a magazine of shipping news. Fleischmann, obliging but not suicidal, turned him down.

On Ross's second attempt he managed to describe his proposed metropolitan weekly with sufficient conviction to win Fleischmann's support. Ross, to Fleischmann's amazement, had not only a well-thought-out editorial concept but also an astute and compelling business plan. His magazine would deliver to metropolitan advertisers the highest number of well-heeled, well-educated readers at the lowest per capita rate. The generally admiring 1934 analysis of *The New Yorker* in *Fortune* magazine claimed that Ross's ideas were so good that it was only a matter of time before someone else would have thought of them. Perhaps, but if Ross must share credit with others for the editorial success of his brainchild, the credit for the brilliant business concept that lay behind it seems to be his alone.

Having drawn up his famous prospectus and set a publication date, Ross began hiring a skeleton staff. He started with his old pal Tyler Bliss from *The Stars and Stripes*, and hired Bliss's wife, Gladys Unger, to operate the switchboard. He hired a young woman named Helen Mears as his secretary.

He also hired an ad salesman with more optimism than common sense, and a secretary for him. This small staff was completed with the addition of a young, aggressive P.R. man, Philip Wylie, who did everything else that had to be done.

Ross wanted his magazine not only to read well but to have a distinctive look. There would be original art on the cover every week reflecting the pace and excitement of metropolitan life. Cartoons would be topical and well drawn. There would be caricatures, and sketches of life in and around the great city. To set the proper tone and help him work his way through the anticipated avalanche of art submissions, Ross hired the former art editor of *Life* magazine, Rea Irvin. In addition to acting as an art adviser to Ross, Irvin designed both an original typeface for the headings in the magazine and logos for the various departments. Ross now had everything but a name.

An informal contest, with the prize of shares, was announced within his circle, and shortly a P.R. friend named John Peter Toohey suggested to Ross *The New Yorker*. It seemed to fit.

On February 17, 1925, the first issue of *The New Yorker* appeared on the newsstands. It was a premature birth, and over the next two years Ross, and a constantly changing staff of associates, struggled valiantly to keep the baby alive.

January 19, 1925

To the Advisory Editors:

The undersigned is deeply grateful to all concerned for the use of their names and advises that he is cognisant of the obligation thereby assumed to get out a publication which will not be scandalously bad....

Mr. Irvin has drawn a wonderful cover for the first issue and as soon as more art material etc. is set up, a dummy will be placed on exhibition at a tea or something.

Sincerely yours,
H. W. Ross

Judge

In 1924 Harold Ross's proposal to publish an illustrated satirical weekly reflecting metropolitan life seemed like a reasonable bet. Over the previous five years Ross had been well positioned to study the competition. There were the humorous weeklies *Judge* and *Life*. Founded in the late 1800s, they were both still profitable though becoming long in the tooth. *Judge* had a pronounced political bias—Republican—while the more elegantly produced *Life* magazine chronicled the rituals and diversions of the wealthy and socially prominent. Both featured short satirical pieces, numerous anecdotes, and comic drawings. The cartoons were of the established "he/she" type. (These were sketches either elaborately stylized or numbingly realistic, illustrating a short, supposedly comic exchange.) In 1924 Charles Dana Gibson purchased *Life* magazine and replaced art editor Rea Irvin with a friend of his own, inadvertently making available to Harold Ross his most important associate in creating *The New Yorker*. There was also *Smart Set*, which was then being edited by George Jean Nathan and H. L. Mencken. Smart it was, but visually drab, and to Ross's taste, and the taste of the general public, too literary and polemical.

Voice from the Wreck—WHY IN THE NAME OF HEAVENS DON'T YOU WATCH WHAT YOU'RE DOING?

Unskilled Equestrian (apologetically)—QUITE RIGHT, OLD CHAP, I ENTIRELY AGREE WITH YOU! BUT DO SPEAK TO MY HORSE ABOUT IT, WON'T YOU? I HAVEN'T ANY INFLUENCE OVER HIM AT ALL.

Mrs. Gayby—YOU WERE SUCH A CHARMING DEBUTANTE, MY DEAR, FIFTEEN YEARS AGO—

Miss Golitely—AND YOU WERE SUCH A CHARMING CHAPERON FOR ME WHEN I CAME OUT.

FIRST STEEL WORKER: *I saw a very unusual issue of a comic magazine the other day, Joe.*

SECOND STEEL WORKER: *What was so unusual about it, Jim?*

FIRST STEEL WORKER: *It didn't contain a single picture of a couple of steel workers wisecracking on a skyscraper.*

HE: *Quitting now? Why, we've only played three holes!*

SHE: *Certainly—par is forty-one, isn't it? And I've already made that!*

"Porter, please tell the engineer not to go around any more corners until I get my clothes off."

The art on these two pages is from *Vanity Fair*. The caricatures are by Miguel Covarrubias, the cover illustration (top right) is by Jacques Darcy, and the illustration bottom left is by Frans Masereel.

ED WYNN   ANN PENNINGTON

A Synthetic City Tragedy
The Whirl of a Great Metropolis

Finally, there was *Vanity Fair*. It announced in its first issue, "We shall not lack authority in those things which go to make the smart world smart." *Vanity Fair* was elegantly edited by Frank Crowninshield and particularly notable for its caricatures and photographs. It had the sophisticated tone Ross longed for. Benchley had been managing editor and Dorothy Parker, Robert Sherwood, and Alexander Woollcott were contributors, but its tone was cosmopolitan, and left Ross the opportunity of focusing on Manhattan life. Its talented editor Crowninshield was known to be held on a short leash by the publisher, Condé Nast, a mistake that Ross was determined not to repeat. Although *Vanity Fair* was beautifully laid out and featured artwork of all kinds, it ran few cartoons in the twenties. (This did seem to pick up in the thirties, perhaps in response to *The New Yorker*'s success in that area.) Ross felt that his edge, as he viewed the competition, would be his magazine's celebration of life in New York. "*The New Yorker* is a magazine avowedly published for a metropolitan audience and thereby will escape an influence which hampers most national publications. It expects a considerable national circulation, but this will come from persons who have a metropolitan interest."

IRVING BERLIN

GLORIA SWANSON

MAKING THE CHEES MO'
BINDING

Skiddle up skat!
Skiddle up skat!
Oh, skiddle up, skiddle up,
Skat, skat! skat!

DOING THE "SCRONCH"

(Left) He, clapping, and singing
   Ron kutta tung
   Ron ka tung
She, feet firmly set on the ground, bending
and swaying

THE NEW YORKER

∎ ∎ ∎

THE NEW YORKER will be a reflection in word and picture of metropolitan life. It will be human. Its general tenor will be one of gaiety, wit and satire, but it will be more than a jester. It will not be what is commonly called radical or highbrow. It will be what is commonly called sophisticated, in that it will assume a reasonable degree of enlightenment on the part of its readers. It will hate bunk.

As compared to the newspaper, The New Yorker will be interpretive rather than stenographic. It will print facts that it will have to go behind the scenes to get, but it will not deal in scandal for the sake of scandal nor sensation for the sake of sensation. Its integrity will be above suspicion. It hopes to be so entertaining and informative as to be a necessity for the person who knows his way about or wants to.

The New Yorker will devote several pages a week to a covering of contemporary events and people of interest. This will be done by writers capable of appreciating the elements of a situation and, in setting them down, of indicating their importance and significance. The New Yorker will present the truth and the whole truth without fear and without favor, but will not be iconoclastic.

Amusements and the arts will be thoroughly covered by departments which will present, in addition to criticism, the personality, the anecdote, the color and chat of the various subdivisions of this sphere. The New Yorker's conscientious guide will list each week all current amusement offerings worth-while—theaters, motion pictures, musical events, art exhibitions, sport and miscellaneous entertainment—providing an ever-ready answer to the prevalent query, "What shall we do this evening?" Through The New Yorker's Mr. Van Bibber III, readers will be kept apprised of what is going on in the public and semi-public smart gathering places—the clubs, hotels, cafes, supper clubs, cabarets and other resorts.

Judgment will be passed upon new books of consequence, and The New Yorker will carry a list of the season's books which it considers worth reading.

There will be a page of editorial paragraphs, commenting on the week's events in a manner not too serious.

There will be a personal mention column—a jotting down in the small-town newspaper style of the comings, goings and doings in the village of New York. This will contain some josh and some news value.

The New Yorker will carry each week several pages of prose and verse, short and long, humorous, satirical and miscellaneous.

The New Yorker expects to be distinguished for its illustrations, which will include caricatures, sketches, cartoons and humorous and satirical drawings in keeping with its purpose.

The New Yorker will be the magazine which is not edited for the old lady in Dubuque. It will not be concerned in what she is thinking about. This is not meant in disrespect, but The New Yorker is a magazine avowedly published for a metropolitan audience and thereby will escape an influence which hampers most national publications. It expects a considerable national circulation, but this will come from persons who have a metropolitan interest.

The New Yorker will appear early in February
The price will be: Five dollars a year
Fifteen cents a copy

Advisory Editors

RALPH BARTON	GEORGE S. KAUFMAN
HEYWOOD BROUN	ALICE DUER MILLER
MARC CONNELLY	DOROTHY PARKER
EDNA FERBER	LAURENCE STALLINGS
REA IRVIN	ALEXANDER WOOLLCOTT

H. W. ROSS, *Editor*

"I am convinced, Joe, that
the country is fundamentally sound."

"The trouble with you, Bill, is
you got your head in the clouds."

"It comes down to this, Bill—
women are less sheltered than they used to be."

And That's That

Ross's ambition was to present the city in all its aspects, from the man in the boardroom to the man in the street (and occasionally, as in this series of Otto Soglow drawings, the man under the street). Ross declared that his magazine "expects to be distinguished by its illustrations, which will include caricatures, sketches, cartoons, humorous and satirical drawings, in keeping with its purpose."

In 1924 Ross was looking for an artist to help him design the first issues of the magazine. Rea Irvin was recommended by Arthur Samuels, whom Fleischmann had hired to run the business side of the operation. When Ross persuaded Irvin to join him at the fledgling magazine, Irvin already had behind him a substantial career as a designer, cartoonist, and illustrator. (Irvin seems to have accepted on a lark. He fully expected the magazine to fail.)

Rea Irvin, posing as Buddha, during the theatrical phase of his career

Born in San Francisco in 1881, Irvin, like Ross, was an only child. He began his professional career as a newspaper cartoonist there and shortly after moved to Honolulu, where he was stranded when the paper went bankrupt, and had to stow away on a freighter to return home. Back in the States he temporarily put aside his career as an artist to pursue one as a member of a traveling stock company. He played the piano, packed the props, painted scenery, and occasionally assumed an acting role. At one point he also performed in films. Irvin had a natural dramatic flair and looked and dressed more like a matinée idol than an artist.

When Irvin resumed his art career after the turn of the century, he finally came east to work on a comic strip for the New York *American*. He became a regular contributor to *Life* magazine and eventually its art editor. His work appeared regularly both in and on the most popular magazines of the day and, equally important, he knew everyone of consequence in the field. For *The New Yorker* he would produce hundreds of spots, cartoons, spreads, and covers—at one point in the lean, early years, four covers in a row. His most widely recognized creation, of course, was the Regency dandy, later dubbed Eustace Tilley, who appears each year on our anniversary cover. Tilley is based on a sketch of the well-known dandy Comte d'Orsay. (It also strangely echoes the cover of a nineteenth-century humor magazine called *The Chap-Book*.) At first and even second look this cover seems an odd choice for Ross's hip, smart-alecky new magazine. In fact, Ross had earlier commissioned a cover which was unsuccessful, and at the last minute he asked Irvin to come up with something that "would make the subscribers feel that we've been in business for years and know our way around."

Irvin had already used a similar figure in his design for several column heads, so it was a simple matter to redo it as a cover. The butterfly that he added is, one assumes, the butterfly of fashion, but the supercilious expression hardly seems appropriate to the freewheeling magazine Ross de-

scribed in his prospectus. Oddly, no one ever asked Irvin why he selected this image, or asked Ross why he agreed to publish it.

Rea Irvin's disposition was as sunny and well balanced as the Japanese prints he so admired. As urbane as Ross was lumpish, he brought to *The New Yorker* exactly the qualities of sophistication and worldliness that Ross was seeking. Irvin's contributions have been freely acknowledged by everyone from Ross on down, but the story of Irvin and *The New Yorker* continues to have several large, tantalizing holes. From 1925 to 1951 Irvin met with Ross every Tuesday afternoon to go through the week's submissions of covers, cartoons, cartoon ideas, caricatures, and illustrations. On Wednesdays Irvin returned to the magazine to follow through on any unfinished art business. (According to William Maxwell, who worked with the artists in the thirties, Wednesdays were usually given over to selecting spot drawings.) In return for this, Irvin received a modest salary, eighty dollars, half in cash and half in stock. (He was receiving the same amount when he retired in 1951.) What Irvin did *not* do for the magazine was meet with the artists. He was well aware of the difficulties even the most talented had in making a living, and he did not have the heart to deliver the bad news that inevitably followed the weekly art meeting. As a consequence, a deputy from the art meetings actually met with the artists. Philip Wylie handled this chore in 1925–26. It was then passed on to Katharine Angell or one of her assistants in the fiction department. This peculiar arrangement had much to do with the evolution of the magazine's art department, and it continued until James Geraghty joined the staff in 1939.

Ross had strong opinions of his own, but he seems to have accepted Irvin's lead in critiquing, correcting, and purchasing drawings. Irvin's style was diplomatic, not peremptory. He provided theoretical support for Ross's intuitive enthusiasm for Helen Hokinson and Peter Arno. He was not infallible, however. William Steig was not his cup of tea, and he did not share E. B. White's enthusiasm for the doodles of James Thurber.

CRITIQUE

Part of a letter from Wylie to James Thurber dated January 3, 1958

The most interesting unanswered question about Irvin and Ross was the extent of Irvin's involvement in the weekly layout of the magazine. This question is not directly dealt with in the books by Thurber, Jane Grant, or Dale Kramer. Grant does describe evenings with Ross, studying the layouts of other magazines—*Life, Punch, Judge,* as well as Continental magazines, like *Simplicissimus.* Surely Ross had some say in the magazine's design, but it's difficult to believe he had the time to do it himself. On the other hand, it's unlikely that Irvin, after spending four or five hours editing with Ross, was asked to pick up the pastepot and lay out the next week's issue. It is possible, of course, that Ross and Irvin considered layouts on Wednesday mornings, but there seems to be no record of such discussions. The printer could have assumed this responsibility, but given Ross's concern for the look of the magazine, that possibility seems remote. There is one other, admittedly unlikely, candidate: the person who has left us a first-hand account of these early art meetings, Philip Wylie. Wylie was the third man in the art meetings from 1925 to 1927. In 1958, in response to Thurber's pieces on Ross, which were then running in *The Atlantic Monthly* magazine, he wrote Thurber a long letter about his early days at *The New Yorker.* (This letter was graciously drawn to my attention by Thomas Kunkel, author of the recently published biography of Ross, *Genius in Disguise.*) Wylie's letter is an attempt to persuade Thurber of Irvin's importance to the creation of Ross's magazine, an importance he feels has not been duly acknowledged. He does mention in passing preparing the magazine for press on Wednesday evenings (Wylie occasionally improvised short bits of verse to fill holes in the copy), but the focus of the

So I was the first one on the NYer to do Ross' firing for him. It raised his estimation of me. He put me in charge of the art department.

I ran it -- meaning I saw the artists all week as they arrived -- attended the Tuesday "art conference" -- with Ross and Re Irvin -- held up the drawings, one by one, and -- with the passage of time -- began to enter the lively -- you can imagine -- discussions about said pictures and captions. I also saw the same artists when they came back, the week following, to collect their myriad rejections -- and/or, rejoice over a $10 or $25 acceptaince of a captionless "spot","tailpiece", or "idea drawing" -- with or without caption.

The point I want to make that really matters, Jim, is this:

It was Rea Irvin, more than everybody else put together, who taught the corny-gag editor-hobo from (I thought it was Idaho) the difference between corn -- and Ross' constantly expressed wish: for a magazine of "sophistication", "satire" etc,, "not for the old lady in Dubuque" -- Ross' slogan.

5

Things like this had happened:

Curtis Arnoux (sp?) Peters showed up, wearing sneakers,
with some drawings signed Arno. We bought one of the
first batch -- a titleless night street scene in which
Arno had gotten the effect of perspective by dropping
regularly-diminished blobs of white paint -- as street
lights -- on his crayon scene.

Arno had idea trouble.* So did Reggie Marsh, who was ~~there~~ an early contributor.
The mobile-stabile guy (can't think of his name though
he wrote me a sputnik-scared letter this summer -- yes --
Alex Calder) drew a few. And he had ideas. So did Otto
Soglow -- before his Little King. I took to buying ideas
-- (after we discussed the proposition on a Tuesday)--
from artist (a) and giving them to (b). I thought up
quite a few scores, myself. In one issue, indeed, all
the "idea" and "caption" drawings were mine, as ideas,
captions.

Hokinson, with her chicken-yard voice, her birth-mark,
some samples of fashion drawings, and two wash-and-line
pictures of two middle-aged ladies, plump butts to
camera, waving farewell handkerchiefs across what was
plainly a dock embarkation fence -- got Irvin raves.
She did some more. I began to think up captions for her.
I also sent -- and took -- her around. Once, for instance,
to Princeton for a football game, which she'd never seen.
In some fall, 1925 issue, there's XXXXXXXXXXXX that;
a full page of how huddles and T-formations looked to Helen;

Johann Bull walked in. Covarrubias came in soon after arriving
from Mexico. Other good carricaturists, to illustrate
"Profiles" -- where Covarrubias drew, the first time,
I think, eyes as spirals.

a full page pix

My "ideas" were, at first, of a localized "Judge-Life"
sort -- pleasing Ross, but not Irvin, much. Thus Reggie
drew one; of a man looking from a ship's porthole at a raging
sea saying, "My God! Belasco must be aboard!" Later, as
I grew in understanding, and Ross did, through Rea, ~~the~~ my
aim and calibre changed.

One day while looking through Arno's weekly portfolio
of offerings, I came upon ~~to raging, trampling~~ two half-shot, bellowing old
bats about to charge obliviously into a trap -- made by
the rise of a sidewalk elevator, under ~~which~~ Arno had
written, "Tripe? I'd do almost anything for a bit o' tripe!"

It greatly amused me. Arno rather uncomfortably said he
hadn't meant to show it -- just something he knocked ~~out~~ off
I showed it. There, the "Whoops Sisters" began -- and
for them I produced dozens of ideas -- finally wrote idly
the story for Arno's book about them.

* Or was lazy! He occasionally came up with a dilly.

"Well, how's Connecticut?"
"All right, but it gets dark
awfully early up there these days."

letter is on Irvin's contributions, not Wylie's. Wylie describes the minuscule staff and his responsibilities within it. These included logging in the art, making notes at the art meeting, and relaying Ross's and Irvin's comments to the artists. He also held the drawings up at the meeting for Ross and Irvin to examine. He was the first "art boy." It is Wylie's contention that these weekly tutorials with Ross not only educated Ross's eye but set a standard of excellence which Ross tried to emulate in the prose of the magazine. He quotes Ross as saying, "Get the prose in the magazine like the art." This may seem far-fetched, but in fact, notes written by Ross at the time—that is, in '25 and '26—seem to suggest that Ross did indeed feel that the art was closer to his vision of the magazine than the text. He wrote to a reader (June 25, 1925): "We are pleased with the magazine's artwork and the generally favorable commentary which the rigid criticism of Rea Irvin and the excellent work of contributors both combined to make possible." In another note dated October 15, 1925: "Everybody talks of *The New Yorker's* art, that is its illustrations. . . . Our text is not as good as it ought to be but I guess it will get better." Ross also had a few things to say to potential contributors, and I think these are worth noting. "By humorous we do not mean comic stuff, captioned by a wisecrack, no custard pie slapstick stuff. We want our things to be humorous from a sophisticated viewpoint. We still accept some purely decorative artistic drawings but less of the former type." He also said, "We want to record the situations of everyday life among intelligent and substantial people as do the English magazines, notably *Punch*, except that our bent is more satirical, sharper." The standard rejection notice read, "The drawings do not quite fit into the art style in which *The New Yorker* will specialize."

If all this is true, it raises another interesting question. Just what art was

Ross talking about? It was certainly not the art of *The New Yorker* as most people understand it today. *The New Yorker* cartoons had not yet been invented. Over the first year, the cartoons averaged less than two an issue, and over the second year the number barely doubled. The covers were bold but not groundbreaking. What *was* being published those first months was a rich and varied range of illustrations, satiric sketches, spots, and caricatures.

The painter Reginald Marsh was contributing sketches and drawings for the "Talk of the Town" section, as were Peggy Bacon and Constantin Aladjalov. Ralph Barton, Miguel Covarrubias, and Al Frueh produced weekly caricatures for the theatre page. (Frueh was an extremely prolific artist. He also did covers, spots, and many notable comic sequences, including his famous study of the volcanic Fiorello La Guardia at City Hall.) A young artist named Julian De Miskey, whose reputation undoubtedly suffered from his decision to sign his innumerable covers and drawings simply "M," was another staple of the early days, as was Johan Bull, who provided the first drawings for the "Talk of the Town" section. (De Miskey soon took over the chore of providing these decorations for "Talk" and created the style that was later refined and perfected by Otto Soglow.) Comic drawings were contributed by Gardner Rea, Rea Irvin, John Held, Jr., and less familiar cartoonists such as I. Klein, Ed Graham, and E. McNerney, Jr. Hans Stengel also did occasional cartoons and caricatures and illustrated an excruciatingly arch series of moral tales in verse called "Our Sermons on Sin." W. Heath Robinson, whose drawings foreshadowed Rube Goldberg, provided full-page whimsies on subjects as diverse as hairdressers and duck hunters. Of the few gags published, most were of the familiar "he/she" variety—that is, a few lines of dialogue, usually between a man and a woman, illustrated with a drawing of the scene.

"The man who marries my daughter will win a prize."
"Well, I must say that's awfully sporting of you."

William Childs

Ross and Irvin struggled to give this hodgepodge some focus, but the early magazines are difficult to look at. The satire ranges from sophomoric to incomprehensible, and the "sophisticated" gags seem to have been lifted from *Captain Billy's Whiz Bang*. If some individual pieces were distinctive, the overall impression was confusion and indecision.

"Merry Christmas, Meadows."
"Merry Christmas, sir. Will that
be all for the present, sir?"
"That will be all, Meadows."
"Thank you, sir."

The New Safety Fork Adjustment for Automobiles
for the Protection of Chickens on the Road

"It's pants matching now, huh? The last time it was permanent waves. What's the idea? Like the pants-matching game better?"

"Naw, it ain't that. I guess it's just that I'm a restless soul, that's all."

Director (shouting): "Make it hot, Alfonso!"
Cinema Hero (with emotion): "I just bought a new town car."
Heroine (swooning): "Not me, I put my dough in real estate."

Heroes of the Week

Ralph Barton

GEORGE V. McLAUGHLIN—*Whose first statement as Police Commissioner set forth his resolution to close up the night clubs at three in the morning. This is the regulation new Police Commissioner's first statement, night clubs being infinitely less difficult to apprehend than the banditti.*

REMO BUFANO—*Who is the creator and the master of the life-size marionettes which replaced the singers in "El Retablo de Maeso Pedro," given last week at the Town Hall under the auspices of the League of Composers. Signor Gatti-Casazza please note.*

TEX RICKARD—*Who has flooded and frozen the floor of his New Garden, reviving for New York the practically extinct game of hockey. A number of people have given up their Charleston lessons to cheer the elusive puck.*

He: *"I can hardly recognize myself in that picture of us leaving the church."*
She: *"No wonder! The stupid newspaper has used a picture of my former wedding."*

Drawn by Hanley.

"Pa, what's all this talk about Evolution?"
"Son, I'll have to consult my attorney before I can
answer that question. I might be sent to jail for it."

GEMS FROM "SUNNY"
The Last Word in Musical Shows at the New Amsterdam
Mary Hay and Clifton Webb stepping a measure in the magnificent
entertainment which stars Marilyn Miller and serves Jack Donahue so well
as an implement of hilarity.—R. B.

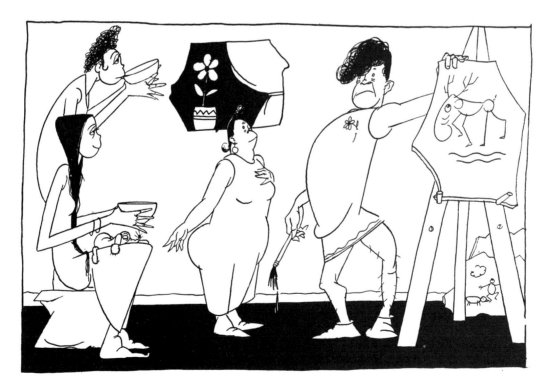

Blessed be the artist for he feeds
The soul with beauty which it needs.
Where genius lets its fires roar
Are always ladies, who adore

The symptoms of his malady
At five o'clock with toast and tea.
Behold, above, the early start
Of noble prehistoric art.—Hans Stengel

The Carramba Quadruplets at Work Training "Plankwalker" and "Jennie Lind," Blue Ribbon Porcupines on THE NEW YORKER'S *Quill Farm. Our Mr. Eustace Tilley, Field Superintendent in Charge of Porcupines, May Be Seen in the Background*

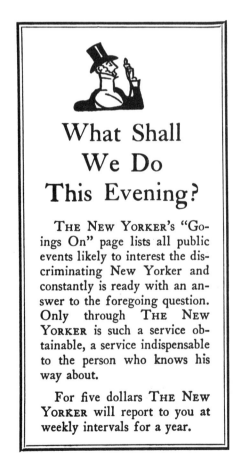

What Shall We Do This Evening?

THE NEW YORKER'S "Goings On" page lists all public events likely to interest the discriminating New Yorker and constantly is ready with an answer to the foregoing question. Only through THE NEW YORKER is such a service obtainable, a service indispensable to the person who knows his way about.

For five dollars THE NEW YORKER will report to you at weekly intervals for a year.

Ross had banged the publicity drums for his new magazine loudly and effectively, and the first printing of fifteen thousand copies was quickly sold out. The next week's issue sold eight thousand copies. By the end of the first month circulation was down to five thousand, and shrinking. The magazine was running from twenty-four to thirty-two pages and the few pages of advertising were usually complimentary. The inside front cover, the prime advertising position, was usually occupied by a full-page sketch. In retrospect, Ross's problems seem clear enough. He had sold Fleischmann the concept for a magazine, but he had rushed into publication before he had fleshed it out. The impressive editorial contributors listed on the magazine's masthead contributed little or nothing. Years later, Ross admitted that this list was in fact "the only dishonest thing [he'd] ever done."

While Ross was furiously bailing out his leaky vessel, the friends he expected to come to his aid were lounging on the dock and enjoying the spectacle. Dorothy Parker did not contribute regularly until 1927. Ross's pal Alexander Woollcott began his celebrated "Shouts and Murmurs" department in 1929, and Robert Benchley took over the theatre section in the same year.

The artwork ranged from brilliant to hum-drum, and the promised satiric features were familiar and flat. The note of sophisticated urbanity that Ross longed for continued to elude him, and the vague but identifiable air of desperation began to rise from the pages of the magazine. What happened in May of 1925 seems to be in dispute. Some accounts suggest that Fleischmann called the staff together to announce the closing of the

Drawings on pages 24 and 25 by Johan Bull

magazine. Later in the day he and Ross met again at a party hosted for Franklin P. Adams's wedding, and the conviviality of the occasion seems to have been contagious. At the end of it Fleischmann decided to give the magazine a new lease on life. Another, more plausible version is that Fleischmann, after seeking a professional appraisal of the magazine's prospects, told Ross he was prepared to float him for another eight months. (How anyone connected to the magazine business could believe that a magazine could be deemed either a failure or a success within such a short period of time remains a mystery.) In any event, Ross and Fleischmann agreed to husband their small resources and plunge forward. The weekly budget was cut from eight thousand to five thousand dollars (Ross sliced his own salary in half), and a large publicity promotion was planned for the fall, including sixty thousand dollars' worth of newspaper advertising. The writer Corey Ford was hired to produce a facetious history of *The New Yorker*, and it began to run inside the magazine as a promotional feature. (In a way this was a forerunner of today's advertorials.) The drawings that accompanied this feature, done by Johan Bull, put the spotlight on Rea Irvin's cover creation and showed him performing various tasks around the magazine. Had Corey Ford not decided to feature this figure, whom he dubbed Eustace Tilley, in this series of promotional pieces, it's likely that today he would be remembered only as a period curiosity, somewhat like Peter Arno's mysterious Whoops Sisters.

THE NEW YORKER'S
Mr. Eustace Tilley, himself

Our moving picture reviewer is here depicted dashing off a dirty crack with the assistance of Mustapha, a prop attendant. Before him are several symbolic dolls, an ingenious galaxy designed by our Mr. Eustace Tilley (who may be seen in the background) for the purpose of reducing the mental level of a contributor to a low enough plane for such a task. After his menial labor, the movie reviewer will be served pâté de fois gras and watermelons and allowed to play with our goldfish.

"The hussy—she says 'I'll give yuh a ring'—then she asks me 'is yer phone number under yer own name?' Lordy!"

"Whoops! Wha' did she think it was under—yer bust measure?"

That Ross was indefatigable is universally acknowledged. That he was a genius is widely conceded. That he was lucky beyond all reasonable expectation is a plain statement of fact. While Ross and his small staff were struggling to revive the failing magazine, three people who would make all the difference appeared over the space of a few weeks.

The first was Peter Arno. A Yale man from a well-to-do family, Arno seems to satisfy everyone's notion of what a *New Yorker* cartoonist should be. He was tall, dark, and handsome; witty, sophisticated, and a crack shot with the ladies. To kill time while he waited for a prospective engagement with a jazz band, he dropped off a few sketches at *The New Yorker*'s offices. Ross, with perhaps a little prodding from Irvin, bought one and encouraged Arno to continue. Although Arno's first *New Yorker* pieces—spot drawings—had vitality, there was little to suggest the bravura style that he would develop over the next few years.

Shortly afterward a young woman named Helen Hokinson appeared at *The New Yorker*'s offices. Hokinson's approach to the magazine was as determined as Arno's was casual. And while Arno's distinctive style still lay ahead of him, Helen Hokinson seems to have arrived fully formed. Coming upon her first quiet, perfect sketches in the sideshow atmosphere of Ross's early magazine is like being handed a glass of cool water in a steam bath. Ross and Irvin knew a good thing when they saw it, and they published Hokinson's drawings as often as possible.

The third and perhaps the most significant addition to the staff was a striking young woman of rare intelligence, patrician bearing, and extraor-

ART CONFERENCE

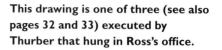

This drawing is one of three (see also pages 32 and 33) executed by Thurber that hung in Ross's office.

THE FUNNY PICTURE IS REJECTED BECAUSE YOU CAN'T TELL WHO IS TALKING, THE OLD LADY OR THE FIREMAN, AND BECAUSE WE HAD A PICTURE OF A MAN TRYING TO GET A DRINK AT A DAM. BESIDES, HOW DID THE OLD LADY GET THROUGH THE POLICE LINES?

dinary self-confidence named Katharine Angell. Katharine Angell was directed to the magazine by a neighbor near her summer home in Sneden's Landing named Fillmore Hyde. Mr. Hyde was at that time editing casuals—short fiction—for Ross, and he recommended Angell to him as a first reader of unsolicited material. Although she received a gloomy assessment of the magazine's prospects from her friend Henry Seidel Canby, then the editor of *The Saturday Review of Literature*, his remarks did nothing to discourage her. Ross was overwhelmed and hired her on the spot.

Of this fateful meeting, E. B. White, who was to become her husband in 1929, had this to say in an interview published in *The Paris Review*: "No two people were ever more different than Mr. Ross and Mrs. Angell. What he lacked, she had. What she lacked, he had. She complemented him in a way that, in retrospect, seems to me to have been indispensable to the survival of the magazine. She was a product of Miss Winsor's and Bryn Mawr. Ross was a high school dropout. She had a natural refinement of manner and speech. Ross mumbled and bellowed and swore. She quickly discovered, in this fumbling and impoverished new weekly, something that fascinated her. Its quest for humor, its search for excellence, its involvement with young writers and artists."

Katharine White with Thurber and friend at Sneden's Landing

"It is then obvious, ladies, that though we may not all be beautiful, we can all be smart."

Helen Hokinson's drawings seem as effortless and natural as the song of a bird, so it comes as a surprise to learn how hard she worked to master her craft. She was clearly gifted as a child, and her parents bravely—and wisely, as it turned out—allowed her to leave her home of Mendota, Illinois, to study art in Chicago. She had early success there as a fashion artist, and that led her to the still wilder shores of Manhattan. Here she continued to freelance, one of her jobs being to produce a comic strip called "Sylvia in the Big City" for the New York *Daily Mirror*. She always claimed that the turning point for her art was an evening sketch class led by Howard Giles. It was there that she was introduced to Hambridge's theory of dynamic symmetry (a system based on a mathematical analysis of classical Greek art). Whatever the catalyst, the figure sketches that filled her notebooks suddenly seemed to breathe life. It was these sketches that she brought in to show Harold Ross at *The New Yorker*. They had distinction, directness, and most importantly for Ross, honesty. Her

"Approach, women of Athens!"

"You'd think George and Ella would try to patch things up for the children's sake."

distinctly configured club women appeared early on, but their beguiling earnestness wasn't revealed until James Reid Parker, her collaborator for many years, allowed us to overhear them speaking. His contribution to her success—he provided captions for almost all of her published work—is impossible to overestimate. It is instructive, however, to contrast these club women with the similarly shaped but temperamentally distinct women whom Helen Hokinson drew for her cover pieces. Her matrons were forthright, if misguided; her "cover girls," as she called them, were self-deluding—simpering after cowboys and Valentinos and helpless in the face of life's simplest tasks. Her covers were beautifully drawn and sometimes amusing, but the grit that's indispensable to even the most delicate art is to be found in her black-and-white collaborations with Mr. Parker. Today, her well-upholstered club women have been displaced by their leaner, keener, daughters, but none of these are more determined or single-minded than Hokinson's creations.

"Thank you, Blackstone; you're such a help to mother."

"Gor! Ten cakes o' soap t' wash 'er! Now I ask yuh, didja ever—"

"An' a fire-hose t' rinse 'er off—watch out, dearie! She's wringin' 'erself out. Whoops!"

From his first, rather expressionistic spots to his final cartoon, fittingly depicting a nymph and a satyr, Peter Arno's drawings have kept *The New Yorker*'s testosterone level well above the national average. His own life was as fast-paced and as exuberant as his drawings. Nightclubs were his natural milieu, and his club-hopping, invariably in the company of the most glamorous debutantes of the day, was widely reported in the press. When he died, his daughter refused a reporter's request for anecdotes about her father with these words: "None are repeatable."

Born Curtis Arnoux Peters, the son of a prominent judge, Arno was well-bred, well-educated, and, compared to most of Ross's undernourished associates, well-off. In 1941 he was voted best-dressed man in America. Arno was self-taught as a draftsman. He designed his wardrobe and an automobile for himself. He was also a competent musician—he played piano—a writer and producer of musical revues, and a journalist. He wrote for newspapers, magazines, the Broadway stage, and Hollywood. Oddly enough, the only thing Arno seemed incapable of doing was creating captions for his own drawings. Philip Wylie dreamed up the surreal dialogue for the first appearance of Arno's drunken charwomen, the Whoops Sisters. When they achieved a following, Arno, with Wylie's assistance, produced a novel about their exploits in a Manhattan boarding-house, complete with a runaway orphan, a mysterious inheritance, and a talking elephant. Arno continued to publish drawings here until his death in 1968, but it was the high spirits and unapologetic sensuality of his early work, creating defining images of pre-Depression America, that established his reputation.

Arno was not a modest man, and

"Makes you kind of proud to be an American, doesn't it?"

even his earliest drawings, angular and swaggering, leap off the page and challenge the reader in a manner that we would now characterize as "in your face." As his style matured, the bold outlines sometimes seemed mechanical, but his growing skill at stage-managing his mini-dramas—the dramatic shadows often suggested floodlights set up in the wings—gave even the slightest gags the impact and luminosity of a neon sign.

Arno was not a strong idea man, and dreaming up material for him to draw became a problem. Philip Wylie claims to have written many of Arno's early ideas. Since whatever humor these early cartoons have is in the drawing and not the captions, the question of authorship seems somewhat beside the point.

Arno was difficult to work with, and in his later years he often complained of what he perceived as a lack of support from the magazine's art department. Fortunately, he was blessed with an editor, James Geraghty, as tough-minded and demanding as he was. Geraghty revered Arno, but he was not intimidated by him. He had, after all, created many of Arno's best lines himself, and Arno, though he constantly tugged on the leash, was totally dependent on Geraghty's ability to supply him with fresh and amusing ideas.

For the first few weeks Katharine Angell worked on a part-time basis, but before the month was out she was working full-time and her responsibilities spilled over from the literary side to the artistic side of the magazine. She seemed to be involved in every aspect of its production and soon was sitting in on the weekly art meetings. (Oddly, Philip Wylie does not mention her in his letter to Thurber.)

These Tuesday afternoon gatherings considered all aspects of the magazine's art, but a disproportionate amount of time seems to have been spent on the comic drawings. Ideas were the biggest problem. Few artists created their own, and everyone at the meeting took a crack at improving or improvising captions. In addition to regular contributors, outside cartoonists and gag writers were encouraged to submit, and much of the afternoon was spent reading (and rejecting) their work. These submissions were either rough captioned sketches or simple typewritten ideas. By some accounts they totaled between one and two thousand a week. These figures may seem preposterous, but they are consistent with the current level of cartoon submissions—approximately thirty-five hundred a week.

Ross was a bit of a bully, but he did not like confrontation. After Wylie left the magazine, it became Katharine Angell's responsibility to transmit

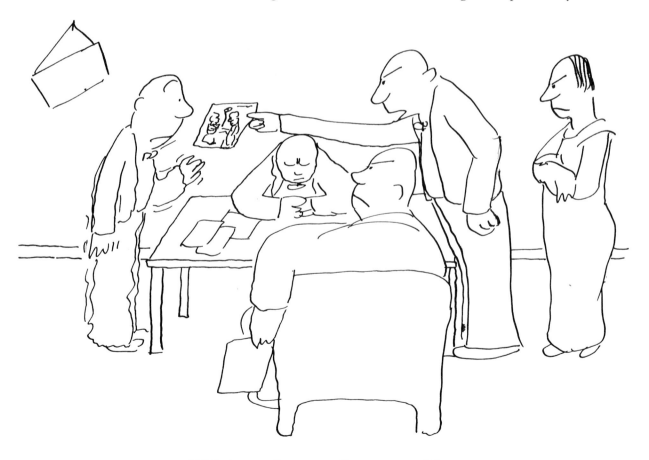

ART CONFERENCE: THE OUTSIDE OPINION:
"Is that funny?"

the results of the weekly meeting to the artists. Presumably Ross believed that bad news would be more tolerable if it were delivered by an attractive woman. Certainly Mrs. Angell had the diplomatic skills that Ross so conspicuously lacked, but she was also a clear-eyed and sometimes brutal critic. Charles Addams once received a rejected cover idea to which one of her memos was still clipped. She described the drawing in question, a piece of whimsy concerning a storm cloud hovering over the weather bureau, as "ghastly in both thought and execution."

Eventually her role as liaison to the artists was delegated to an assistant in the fiction department, Scudder Middleton, then Wolcott Gibbs, and then William Maxwell. She remained a powerful voice in the selection of the magazine's art even after she and her second husband, E. B. White, moved to Maine in the mid-thirties. From both an administrative and editorial perspective, it seems fair to say that at least until the Second World War the art department was essentially a division of the fiction department.

MIDSUMMER ART CONFERENCE

Ross, after fretting over the layout of the magazine for the first few months, finally came up with an arrangement that satisfied him. "Goings On," which had shuttled from the front to the back several times, finally settled in the front. After "Goings On" came "The Talk of the Town," a column of sophisticated gossip. "Talk" was followed by "Behind the News," short features with a metropolitan slant, and "Of All Things," which essentially was the magazine's editorial page. The gossip in "Talk" for which Ross had had high hopes was flat, and reluctantly he dropped it. "Behind the News" and "Of All Things" were combined into one new "Talk" section, which led off with a page of editorial reflections called "Notes and Comment." Ross's solution set the pattern for the front of the book which we followed until 1992, when Tina Brown separated "Notes and Comment" from "Talk" and moved it to the lead-off spot in front of "Goings On."

WHY WE GO TO CABARETS

A Post-Debutante Explains

The stag line is not a collection of which any hostess can be proud.

By the fall of '25 Ross's magazine was improving. There were more drawings, and some of them were actually funny. "A Reporter at Large" by Morris Markey was drawing attention. "Talk," now handled by Fillmore Hyde, was well written and interesting. Potential advertisers, however, remained unimpressed and time was running out. Over the first six months

Ross had assembled some promising ingredients, but the recipe for a successful magazine continued to elude him. Again, good luck rather than inspiration seems to have turned the tide. In November of 1925 the magazine ran a short piece by a young woman named Ellin Mackay from a socially prominent family. Her piece was billed as an "exposé" of Park Avenue society and ran under a headline more appropriate to the *Police Gazette* than *The New Yorker*: "Why We Go to Cabarets: A Post-Debutante Explains." As someone who takes the traditions of the magazine seriously, I'm reluctant to admit that this piece of sensational fluff, not the talents of Ross, Irvin, Hokinson, or Arno, turned people's attention to the magazine. I prefer to believe that this was just an incidental, even freakish event on the road to inevitable success. In any case, shortly after the publication of the Mackay piece, which was front-page news in New York City's three leading daily newspapers, and even before Mackay created further headlines by marrying Irving Berlin against her father's wishes, advertising began flowing into the magazine.

Up to that point, the magazine had been a limp twenty-four pages. Aside from the classified section at the back of the book, the most prominent ads were freebies for the magazine's printer, Powers, and the publisher's relatives, that is, Fleischmann's yeast. The publicity generated by the Mackay article changed all that. By the middle of 1926 the magazine was averaging a hundred pages a week, including ads from Bonwit Teller, Saks Fifth Avenue, and other upscale Manhattan shops. This meant a corresponding increase in the number of editorial pages and created an opportunity for more young artists. The first *New Yorker* cartoon collection, which was published in 1928, included (in addition to the artists already mentioned) Alan Dunn, Perry Barlow, Gluyas Williams, Leonard Dove, and Barbara Shermund. The second album, published the following year, added work by Garrett Price, Don Herold, Carl Rose, Milt Gross, and Mary Petty.

The New Yorker's first anniversary issue was a whopping seventy-two pages, and best of all, twenty of these were advertising. In a bit of justifiable self-congratulation the lead item in "Talk" presented some astonishing statistics. Thirteen hundred and fifty ad pages were under contract for the following year, an average of twenty-six per issue. Circulation was nearing forty thousand. The magazine, which had survived a near-death experience in May eight months earlier, was born again. Assuming that Ross assembled the strongest possible issue for the occasion of its first anniversary, the contents are perhaps worth examining.

The Rivals

Butama Queenie, the Mexican hairless, who weighs two pounds, not counting sweater

THE DOG SHOW

The anniversary issue opened up with "Goings On." After ads by Bonwit's, Saks, and several other upscale retail stores, we come to the "Talk" section, decorated by Johan Bull, a profile of the art dealer Otto Kahn, and "Paris Letter" by Genêt (Janet Flanner). The nightclub scene had been taken over from Charles Baskerville by Lois Long (who signed herself "Lipstick"), and she offered a report on café society. There were also reviews of cinema, theatre, and books, and six pages of sports coverage. The features included a double-page drawing by Rea Irvin, inspired by a recent freak snowstorm, a running feature called "Heroes of the Week," with caricatures by Ralph Barton, Morris Markey's "A Reporter at Large" about a double murder, and a running feature called "Metropolitan Monotypes." There was also light verse, and Ross's pet, a weekly quiz called "Are You a New Yorker?" Finally, there was a promotion piece in the series written by Corey Ford celebrating, facetiously, the magazine's fiftieth birthday.

The issue has heft, it reads well, and it's pleasingly laid out. What is particularly notable about it, however, is what it does not contain: cartoons. Helen Hokinson is represented by a group of sketches from the dog show, and Peter Arno offers merely an illustration for a piece on modern music. The Otto Kahn profile is decorated with a caricature by Hans Stengel, and Johan Bull provides the decorative drawings for Corey Ford's faux promo. The closest thing to a cartoon is Al Frueh's drawing, part of a continuing series, called "Solving the Traffic Problem." The furthest thing from a cartoon is a self-congratulatory birthday card entitled "The Birthday of the Infantus," by an artist named James Daugherty, who signed himself "Jimmy the Ink."

SOLVING
THE TRAFFIC
PROBLEM

Looking back from the nineties or even from the thirties, this lack of cartoons seems astonishing. The truth is, however, that gag cartoons didn't become an important part of the editorial mix until late the following year. Helen Hokinson was yet to begin her lifelong collaboration with James Reid Parker, and Arno had not yet hit his stride. Ross had managed to put his magazine into orbit with a handful of dedicated writers and editors and an even smaller group of artists, most of whom are no longer remembered.

THE BIRTHDAY OF THE INFANTUS

THE NEW YORKER CUTS HIS BIRTHDAY CAKE
THE GUESTS FROM RIGHT TO WRONG — MR. J·S·SUMNER · DR·J·ROACH STRATON
DR·YMCA CADMAN · MERELY MR. BUCKNER · MISS O'LADY D'BUQUE AND THE INFANTUS

Otto H. Kahn

Janet Thurber

"Touché!"

In 1925, while Harold Ross was in Manhattan trying desperately to keep his new magazine afloat, James Thurber was in Columbus, Ohio, trying to support a new marriage. He was doing P.R. work for a list of clients that included a regional circus and the Cleveland Orchestra. The circuitous path that eventually led Thurber to Ross's magazine began later that year when Thurber decided to throw everything over and sail off to France to start a novel. On the crossing, Thurber met a woman who turned out to be E. B. White's sister. He filed away her name—Lillian Illian—not because of her connection to *The New Yorker* but because the name appealed to him. This kind of coincidence seems to happen again and again in the course of the magazine's history. Katharine Angell had come to *The New Yorker* as a result of a casual conversation with a summer-house neighbor, Fillmore Hyde. Peter Arno had wandered by between gigs as a piano player, and Janet Flanner's letters from Paris were an elaboration of informal notes she had been sending to her friend Jane Grant.

After a frustrating summer in Normandy, Thurber abandoned his novel, and he and his wife moved to Paris. He landed a job as a rewrite man on *The Paris Review*. But it was in the paper's rival, the *Herald,* that he once more came across mention of *The New Yorker.* The Ellin Mackay pieces on high society caused shock waves that traveled far beyond Manhattan and landed the story in the pages of the Parisian newspapers.

Thurber spent the end of that year and the beginning of the next working on the Chicago *Tribune*'s Riviera edition. It was pleasant work, but it was not advancing his career, and in '26 he sailed off by himself back to Manhattan, where he took a job on the *Evening Post.* He was again working as rewrite man when Franklin P. Adams devoted an entire "Conning Tower" column to one of Thurber's pieces. Soon after Thurber was promoted to feature editor.

In February of '27 Thurber ran into a young man at a party, and they immediately hit it off. This was another remarkable coincidence, because the young man was E. B. White, who hated parties and seldom attended them. The remarkable friendship between White and Thurber is a story that deserves a book of its own. It's only important to say here that they

immediately took to each other. White encouraged Thurber to try his hand at *The New Yorker*, and he introduced him to Ross. Ross hired him on the mistaken impression that Thurber was an old friend of White's. In many respects, Ross had a remarkably sharp nose for talent, but he seems to have misjudged Thurber from the beginning. He was a gifted, if unformed, writer, but Ross hired him as an editor. He was an artist whose work would bring acclaim to the magazine, but Ross refused to publish his drawings. He was a man of mercurial temperament, who when bored enjoyed knocking things over, but Ross charged him with the task of bringing order to the magazine.

Ross and Thurber did have some things in common. They both loved practical jokes and amusing stories. Thurber was an excellent, sometimes cruel mimic, and a terrific storyteller. He seems to have spent most of his first few months at the magazine, however, trying to get Ross to fire him. He disrupted what routine there was with loud noises. (He once rolled a garbage can down the hall.) And he set a bad example for the rest of the staff by ordering himself a very expensive typewriter when everyone else was sharing pencils. Thurber describes his position at the magazine at the time as managing editor. In fact, that job was held from 1925 to 1930 by Ralph Ingersoll, Jr. It seems more likely that Thurber was what was known as the Sunday Editor, that is, he was responsible for seeing that everything that needed to be available for the following week's issue in fact was. Ross never did fire Thurber, but with the encouragement of E. B. White and Dorothy Parker, he did finally move him from a managerial to an editorial position.

Thurber shared an office with White while working on "The Talk of the Town" and "Notes and Comment." (At the time there were only two private offices at *The New Yorker*. One was occupied by Katharine Angell, the other by Harold Ross himself.) Thurber freely acknowledged his debt as a writer to White, who was five years his junior, and over the next eight years the pieces White and Thurber wrote for "Talk" and "Notes and Comment" established the tone of the magazine's prose: light, elegant, precise, and witty. Thurber's first two pieces were, by the way, not comments or reflections but short poems which appeared in the issue of February 26, 1927. Although the Algonquin Round Table is often talked about as if it were an annex of the magazine itself, its regulars had little to do with shaping *The New Yorker*. Ross did stage-manage one appearance by White and Thurber at these gatherings, but it was not a success. They found the celebrated badinage coarse and self-congratulatory. Neither returned for seconds.

"*All right, have it your way—you heard a seal bark!*"

BIRTH OF A LOVE AFFAIR   DEATH OF A LOVE AFFAIR

Marriages are made in Heaven

Thurber was from childhood a compulsive doodler, and White was charmed by his sketches. He kept pestering Ross to publish them, and Ross kept turning him down. Even Ross admitted later on that this was a failure on his part, but how did it come about? For one thing, Ross, who was full of bluster, was not sufficiently confident of his own eye to take a chance on Thurber. And the ease with which these sketches were dashed off might have made Ross suspect their value. How could anything done so quickly be any good? The fact that Thurber himself tossed most of them into the wastebasket probably reinforced this suspicion. Even so, it seems likely that Ross would have published Thurber if Irvin had championed the idea. Rea Irvin was a virtuoso draftsman and was as demanding of others as he was of himself. Katharine Angell often complained to Ross about the frequency with which Irvin turned down perfectly good material, and Irvin's resistance to William Steig's drawings was such that his work was eventually routed around the art meetings and handled directly through Ross's office. I think we can fairly assume that Irvin was, at best, indifferent to Thurber's style. This would have been enough to discourage Ross, who already felt that Thurber was trying to put something over on him.

Thurber's drawings have been reproduced in both collections of his own work and anthologies drawn from the pages of *The New Yorker*, but for the most part these only hint at the essence of Thurber's genius: his free-flowing, rhythmic line. For purposes of reproduction, the original sketches, quickly dashed off in pencil, were carefully inked in by White (and occasionally Thurber himself), masking the graceful spontaneity of the originals.

The sketches on these pages, tossed off on hotel stationery while on vacation, offer us a unique opportunity to experience directly the masterful graphic shorthand that first attracted White and others to his work.

DIVORCES ARE OKAY IN HELL

A pair of Martinets

The captions for the drawings at the bottom of pages 42 and 43 were written by E. B. White.

Thwarted in his campaign for the Thurber drawings at *The New Yorker*, White strong-armed the publisher of their first joint venture, *Is Sex Necessary?*, to include Thurber's drawings. The book, inspired by several popular works on Freud and sexuality, consisted of alternating chapters by Thurber and White and is considerably enhanced by Thurber's sketches. These were casually drawn in pencil. For purposes of reproduction it was necessary to ink them in. With characteristic insouciance Thurber delegated this chore to White.

The book was an unexpected success, and Ross began to have second thoughts. Thurber's first *New Yorker* drawings appeared in 1930, illustrating a series of facetious pieces offering advice to pet owners, called "Our Pet Department." The frequency with which Thurber's cartoons appeared over the next few years is suggested by the fact that his first collection of drawings, *The Seal in the Bedroom*, published in 1932, contains eighty-five sketches, of which only half were from *The New Yorker*.

White's contribution to the success of these early drawings went beyond cheerleading and occasional inking in. In the Thurber scrapbooks in the *New Yorker* library, many of Thurber's early clips are initialed "E.B.W." According to Helen Stark, retired head of the library, these initials indicate that the captions were actually created by White. This is not as far-fetched as it sounds. White, after all, was the one who salvaged most of Thurber's drawings from the wastebasket, and captioning drawings was a routine part of his job.

"Now I'm going to go in over your horns!"

Among those enthusiastically hailing Thurber's drawings, both here and abroad, was the English painter and critic Paul Nash. He compared Thurber's spontaneous and flowing line to Matisse's. This is perhaps a bit of a stretch, but there is a kind of controlled delirium and exuberance in Thurber's early drawings that sets them apart from anything else in the magazine. Thurber's drawings are sparsely furnished, much of them seemingly assembled from tag sales—a lumpy sofa, unsteady side tables, some ill-matched lamps, and a few prints on the wall. When the action moved outside, the scenery resembles props discarded by a traveling opera company. Thurber's main players—men, women, and beasts—are by most measures anatomically challenged. By the sheer power of their body language, however, they have a reality that transcends mere illustration. Thurber's visual language was economical but concise. He was a master of gesture—the slump of a shoulder or the angle of an eyebrow said all that was necessary, and could convey the most subtle messages of aspiration, desperation, or resignation.

These wonderful drawings did much to consolidate *The New Yorker*'s growing reputation for sophistication. It is one of the many ironies of the history of the magazine that Thurber, who, after all, joined the staff in 1927, was one of the few artists connected with the magazine who found it necessary to establish a reputation elsewhere before he was published in our pages.

The Hopeless Quandary

"It's Lida Bascom's husband—he's frightfully unhappy."

By the mid-thirties, though its monocle was still firmly focused on Manhattan, *The New Yorker* was a national institution. In 1934 *Fortune* magazine ran a long, admiring profile of Ross and his magazine, which examined his success in both commercial and artistic terms. (This unsigned article was written by someone well qualified on the subject—Ralph Ingersoll, Jr., who had been managing editor of *The New Yorker* from 1925 to 1930.) The piece includes a short history of the magazine, biographies of all the major players, and a persuasive and statistic-studded analysis of *The New Yorker* as a business enterprise. Salaries are given. (Thurber and White were pulling down $11,000 a year. Ross was making $40,000 a year plus stock.) There are also ad rates and production costs. The editorial budget in 1934 was $8,000 a week: For art $1,800, for manuscripts $1,800, for departments $1,800, salaries $2,200, miscellaneous $400. Few contributors held stock in the magazine. Ross had 10 percent, Rea Irvin and Katharine White (she had married E. B. White in 1929) less than 5 percent each. The only staff member on the board of directors was, surprisingly, not Ross but Rea Irvin. (Ross bypassed the board and communicated directly with Raoul Fleischmann.)

Ross's ability to deliver a large slice of Manhattan's upper crust to his advertisers was the key to the magazine's prosperity. For $550 a page, *The New Yorker* was reaching sixty-two thousand of the best-heeled customers in the city. By comparison, *The New York Times* could cost $2,131 a page. It was read by a much larger audience, but that audience was more diffuse and less affluent. As evidence of the magazine's phenomenal success, *Fortune* reported that in the first six months of 1934 it ran more ad pages than *The Saturday Evening Post.*

Ingersoll made an effort to define Ross's journalistic philosophy, but in truth his principles were few and mostly negative: No bunk, no flattery, and no mistakes. Keeping his sometimes wayward vessel on course did not leave Ross much time for introspection, a task to which he seems to have been generally unsuited in any case. E. B. White's "Notes and Comment" pieces often suggested some moral compass, but *The New Yorker* carefully avoided articulating a clear editorial position on almost any issue. (It was, however, against Prohibition and in favor of regulating advertising.) But if *The New Yorker* refused to take itself seriously, others did. Many writers and journalists pointed to *The New Yorker* as a model of reportorial balance and accuracy. Surely staff members, all clever, intelligent people, had some thoughts about what kind of magazine they were producing, but they shared these thoughts only with one another.

A curious exception to this rule of silence is to be found in an unexpected place, *The New Yorker*'s seventh cartoon collection. The annual collections of cartoons, and occasionally caricatures, generally appeared with a brief, usually facetious introduction by a staff writer. Benchley, Ring Lardner, Jr., and Thurber all had a go. The book published in 1935 had two introductions. The first, written by the critic Lewis Mumford, laments the shortcomings of *The New Yorker*'s art and is published under the heading "The Undertaker's Garland." The response by Wolcott Gibbs—described as "a partial defense"—was titled "Fresh Flowers." Mumford weighs in with these words: "This is the first time I have ever been asked to deliver an opinion about *The New Yorker*'s art, and if I manage to say half the things I have been thinking these last ten years, it will probably be the last" (it was). He goes on to lambast the drawings as "less interesting than the ideas," characterizing them as too often "elfin, disassociated, abstract." Although he has some kind words about Hokinson, Steig, and Arno, he is disappointed by their failure to capture the faces of contemporary New York. He lists these as "the subway face, the Library face, the luncheon face…the Union Square face…the Ethical Cultural Face." He longs for a Daumier or a Hogarth to produce "wise, swift, mocking accounts of our contemporaries." "*The New Yorker* album," he continues, "should be encrusted with such family portraits, tart, teasing and terrible." He finds instead that the magazine is producing comedy that has "that special kind of temporary madness that springs out of a tough day at the office and three rapid Martinis."

This is rough stuff. *The New Yorker* at that time was publishing (in addition to the artists mentioned above) James Thurber, Mary Petty, Alan Dunn, Gluyas Williams, Reginald Marsh, William Crawford Galbraith, Richard Decker, and Perry Barlow. *The New Yorker* had taken a form of satiric drawing, which at the beginning of the century had degenerated either into banal and predictable editorial cartoons or long-winded and formularized whimsies, and created a fresh, vital new way of commenting on the world in pictures. Mr. Mumford's hindsight was 20/20, but he completely missed a revolution right under his nose. Wolcott Gibbs's response is a straightforward but hardly spirited defense of the artists. He rightly points out that *The New Yorker* is, after all, a business enterprise and that finding the comic art for its pages is a difficult and consuming task. As liaison between the autocrats at the art meetings and the penurious artists, Gibbs got it from both sides. The artists believed he was not sufficiently aggressive in pressing the merits of their work, and the editors felt that the

"A new humor of a finer, more forceful nature (think of those delicate, fine things in some of those Chaplin films, think of Buster Keaton, of Sinclair Lewis).

"Here is something which astonishes the European, because here he discovers a side of the American character with which he is less familiar than with the usual slapstick, rough and tumble American comedy.

"It is not the type of humor that causes loud laughter, but which causes one to smile, because it illustrates a particular situation so definitely and is so true to life. It is American humor, because it is drawn by Americans and bears captions in English. Fundamentally, however, it is human humor, very closely related to the great humorists of Europe, who never grow older because they were never obvious.

"For decades America has seized everything that came from the old continent. Now it is gradually discovering itself."

(Translated from *Die Dame* [Berlin], February 24, 1930)

"Well, there goes Junior."

art suffered from his reluctance to lay on the whip. He put it this way: "From this divided allegiance in fact I have learned nothing beyond an understanding of the technical and emotional difficulties in the production of any drawings whatsoever suitable for magazine publication." While Mumford was calling for madder music and stronger wine, Gibbs was up to his eyebrows in trying to get out Ross's goddamned magazine.

The New Yorker over the years has been blessed with the opportunity to publish drawings and covers by some of the most talented artists of its time. Many of these are also gifted satiric writers, and the body of their work constitutes a social history of our times that is unrivaled anywhere. It's important to note, however, that this work was produced not to fill gaps in Mr. Mumford's pantheon but to put food on the table. Artists have to make a living just like everyone else. To be able to keep oneself off the public dole while producing work that both instructs and delights is a remarkable achievement in any age. What place their efforts will occupy in the still-to-be-established canon of twentieth-century art is unpredictable. Tomorrow's critics, after all, are being weaned on Beavis and Butt-head, not the Whoops Sisters. The magazine's debt to these artists, however, is undeniable, and if their work did not satisfy Mr. Mumford's expectations, the fault lies with, as Gibbs concluded, the editors. "We have done little or nothing toward formulating a coherent political philosophy (beyond the negative one of suspecting all such philosophies) and have I'm afraid practically no intention of beginning now."

"Hey, what about dames?"

SMALL FRY
No Tonsils

"Oop—sorry."

Richard Decker

"Certainly I get tired of it, but it's the only thing I know."

Whitney Darrow Jr.

"How did you happen to find this place?"

The New Yorker has often been criticized for referring to its cartoons as "drawings." This peculiar usage is not an attempt to elevate the tone of either the magazine or its contributors but rather reflects the simple fact that for many years the majority of cartoons published here were collaborations between gag writers and the magazine's artists. The writers supplied the ideas—the artists did the drawings. In addition to staff writers who wrote gags, The New Yorker over the years has supported a large group of outside writers, none as prolific as Richard McCallister, now in his eighty-sixth year. In the course of his career, McCallister provided more than four thousand ideas to the magazine, and at one point he was submitting more than a thousand a year.

Looking back from the present, when few artists would ever consider doing someone else's work, it's difficult to understand how cartoonists as idiosyncratic as Peter Arno, George Price, Helen Hokinson, and Richard Taylor could have been so dependent on others for their material. The gag writer, in fact, emerged from an evolutionary process that began at the turn of the century with the standard ingredient of most comic magazines: the illustrated anecdote. These were usually half a dozen lines long and sometimes ran as long as two or three paragraphs. Essentially they were comic tales, often accompanied by a drawing, usually in an elaborate illustrational style. Over time these were pared down to two or three lines of dialogue, the "he/she joke" that was the standard at the time The New Yorker began publishing. The two-line caption survived into the twenties and occasionally appears today, but The New Yorker has been credited, properly it seems, with nourishing and perfecting the single-line caption.

"Gee, Jack! That was very careless of you."
Idea by R. McCallister

"It's broccoli, dear."
"I say it's spinach, and I say the hell with it."
Idea by E. B. White

Idea by R. McCallister

William Steig and George Price, among others, have told me that this development was recognized and discussed among cartoonists at the time. Just how it came about seems impossible to establish sixty-five years after the fact. I suspect it was the result of the increasing sophistication of the gag writers rather than the cartoonists themselves. It's hard to believe that one man could be responsible for such an innovation, but if a candidate had to be put forward, I would nominate E. B. White. From his first days at the magazine, in 1927, polishing captions was one of his responsibilities, and the gag lines showed an immediate improvement after his arrival. White also produced the "snappers," one-line comments, for the magazine's newsbreaks, and these were often gags in themselves. At the very least his example set a new standard for the gag writers submitting to the magazine. The single-line caption also required a new subtlety on the part of the artist: the less told in the caption, the more one had to tell in the drawing.

Ross thought that the test for comic drawing should be, "Could this have happened?" And in a note from the same period he says, "We insist on the artist putting the idea into the picture rather than into the wording." Another favorite of Ross's at the early art meetings was "Where am I in this picture?" The application of these ideas to *New Yorker* cartoons had, I believe, a lot to do with the increasingly pithy captions and the plausibility of the drawings themselves. This dialectical process between artists and writers eventually resulted in the evolution of a distinctive new cartoon style based more on character than situation which became a prototype for what most people now consider the typical *New Yorker* cartoon.

"He's an amused spectator of the passing show, Sergeant. That's all I can get out of him."
Idea by R. McCallister

"Which one is the love potion?"

"Hmm. Is this some of _our_ work, Madame?"

"You know, Mater, I decided it would be nice if you went to Germany and took some baths."

"Rubbish!
Lots of children
are unwanted. Your father and I didn't want _you_."

Even in the desperate early days, *The New Yorker* had a few artists who produced more new ideas than they could draw themselves. These were eagerly seized on by Ross and re-tooled by the editors to fit the styles of other, less versatile artists. Otto Soglow was one such contributor. Another was Alan Dunn, who began his career here in 1926. Dunn was an excellent draftsman and a student of architecture. His early offhand sketches in conte crayon gradually gave way to more elegant, refined drawings in pen and ink. He continued to contribute clever, often timely ideas to the magazine until his death in the mid-seventies. Dunn was married to Mary Petty. The Dunns were a very private couple. Mary was occasionally seen in the office delivering her work, but Alan never came in. (Ross described him as a recluse-about-town.) Mary first began appearing in our pages in 1927. Although her beautiful and mysterious drawings shared some characteristics of her husband's work, they were, in both conception and execution, uniquely her own. She chronicled a richly imagined world of wealth and privilege presided over by a devoted but eccentric parlor maid, half sylph and half butterfly. Curiously, Alan's work, so much of it topical, has lost most of its edge while Mary's world remains as easy to enter and as hard to leave as it always was.

"If I take the 4:17,
that will get me home in time to gargle at 5."

"The Indians had him completely at bay. He saved his last shot
for your Great-Great-Great Aunt Fanny."

"Darling, let's get drunk."

"It'll be a few minutes before we can shoot. You folks want something to eat?"

As the magazine prospered in the thirties, the variety and range of the comic art in its pages grew. The art at that time can be divided roughly into four categories: the great illustrators—William Crawford Galbraith, Wallace Morgan, Richard Decker, Garrett Price, Carl Rose—most of whom relied on gagmen; the great satirists—Gluyas Williams, Ralph Barton, Al Frueh; the great stylists—Hokinson, Arno, George Price, Steig, Thurber—who created, with or without the help of gagmen, worlds of their own; and the clowns—John Held, Jr., Otto Soglow.

Although representatives of most of these categories survive in today's *New Yorker*, the day of the great comic illustrator seems to be behind us. With the death of Charles Saxon and the retirement of Whitney Darrow,

"All right then, what is your conception of the Awakening of Intelligence through Literature and Music?"

THE SALOON MUST GO!

very few current contributors—Robert Weber, Jim Stevenson, Mischa Richter, and Edward Sorel are exceptions—could produce the elegant full-page tour de force that was a hallmark of these masters of the thirties and forties. No member of the younger generation has either the skill or, it seems, the inclination to continue this tradition. Several factors contribute to this, but I think the primary cause is the emergence of a new, very personal comic sensibility in the sixties and seventies. These artists have now brought an art form that began with a collaboration between writers and artists full circle. Many of them are, it seems to me, essentially writers who illustrate their own pieces. The nuances that often characterized the graphic work of early contributors are now more often to be found in the captions, I think, than in the drawings themselves.

"Well, for the love of God! You're supposed to be on the Santa María waving good-bye."

"If you're so good, why can't you ever strike twice in the same place?"

The elegant simplicity of *The New Yorker*'s early covers can be traced to two sources: Rea Irvin's informed eye and Raoul Fleischmann's shallow pockets. The Deco-derived designs, with their angular shapes and bold flat colors, often suggesting paper cutouts, were eye-catching, but they were also inexpensive to reproduce. The cover of July 11, 1925, which ran when the till was almost empty, was printed in simple black-and-white.

Ross had this to say about the covers in a letter dated August 25, 1925: "Up till now, we feel our covers have been consistently good, but the tone has been rather scattered, due to a wide range of subjects. From now on we feel we should tend strongly toward the elegant. That is to say the fashionable and smart, the dinner jacket rather than the sailor's uniform. Situations built with a background of smart social functions rather than character studies of the lower classes."

Looking through the covers of that first year, I find it difficult to see what Ross meant by character studies of the lower classes. Did Ross mean Al Frueh's cover depicting two muscle-bound policemen patrolling in what appears to be a golf cart? Or the couple necking at the top of the Fifth Avenue bus? Perhaps he was thinking of the cover of May 9, the street cleaner anxiously observing with some embarrassment what seems to be the nuptial flight of two butterflies. (Is this a reference, one wonders, to Eustace Tilley on the first cover?) The De Miskey cover of June 27 shows a family at the beach, but since they are all partially submerged it is impossible to tell if their class is lower, upper, or middle. In fact, until one of Bill Steig's small fry turned up on the cover in 1932, trying to smuggle a large firecracker past an even larger policeman, it's unusual to find anything on the covers to suggest that people in Manhattan had to work for a living.

These earliest covers were produced by artists as dissimilar as Julian De Miskey, H. O. Hofman, Ilonka Karasz, A. E. Wilson, Irvin himself, of course, and James Daugherty. With the signatures removed it would be hard to tell these pieces apart. The overall impression, however, is distinctly upbeat, upscale, and upper-class. Over the next several years the covers gain in variety and richness, but it's not until Hokinson and Arno begin appearing regularly in 1928 and 1929 that one gets a whiff of what the classic *New Yorker* covers would be.

Ross loved running gags, both inside the magazine and on its covers. The Arno drawing, for example, which appeared on the cover on November 27, 1926—a doorman with a rake, waiting for the last leaf to fall—is echoed the following spring, April 9, 1927, by another Arno sketch of the same fellow up on a ladder waiting for the first leaf to unfold. On July 16

of the same year, 1927, Helen Hokinson introduced the empty-headed and sentimental matron who was to be the magazine's longest-running cover feature. Although in configuration virtually indistinguishable from Helen Hokinson's club women, she is of a decidedly different temperament. She pursues romance, not self-improvement. And the ever resourceful butler at her elbow expertly shields her—he baits her hook, he carries her parasol—from the perplexities and burdens of life that so bedevil her sisters. In addition to the butler, her constant companion is a small and embarrassed-looking Scottish terrier. In 1931, presumably to escape the unpleasantness of the Depression, she embarks on an around-the-world cruise, which is

recorded in eleven covers published that year. She survived here until 1949, when we find her not on a transatlantic cruise but on a train making her way in from the suburbs, handing her ticket to the conductor and at the same time trying to hide her dog under a coat.

Rea Irvin himself tried a running series in the thirties. These are beautifully designed and elegantly executed, but it's hard not to feel uncomfortable looking at them today. Rendered in the style of classic Japanese prints, they portray Asians in Western dress trying their hands at Ping-Pong, croquet, poker, horse racing, and hunting. The assumption behind the pieces is that there is something tremendously amusing about the Japanese attempts to emulate Western customs.

By the middle thirties the addition of William Steig, Perry Barlow, William Cotton, Garrett Price, and Richard Decker to the ranks of cover artists was accelerating the movement away from the rigid and highly stylized pieces of the twenties. This trend can be clearly seen in the work of Constantin Alajalov (originally Aladjalov, he presumably dropped the *d* to make his name seem more American). His early work, first published here in 1925, was highly stylized in a manner suggesting the experiments of the Cubists. By the late thirties he was working in a naturalistic style equally appropriate to *The New Yorker* and what was to become his other major market, *The Saturday Evening Post*.

The twenties celebrated Gotham's upper crust and its pleasures; the thirties celebrated the quieter pursuits of the suburban middle class: family sing-alongs replaced cabaret, and softball replaced polo. In 1939 James Thurber, the last word in sophistication, takes us to the ultimate middle-class event, the New York World's Fair.

For George Price, who died this year at the age of ninety-three, drawing pictures was always a greater pleasure than creating cartoons. He conceded that "cartooning is an honorable way to make a living, but it's a contrived thing . . . an illustrated joke." Price had been filling sketchbooks with his characteristic low-lifes, harridans, and sourballs since he was in his early teens. His natural taste for recording the joys and nesting places of the socially marginal was encouraged from an early period by a family friend, the American social-realist painter George "Pop" Hart. Hart worked with Price's father, a carpenter, in what was America's first film capital, Fort Lee, New Jersey. Price Senior built movie sets and "Pop" Hart painted them.

George seemed to have spent all of his free time sketching, either with "Pop" Hart—a picnic park along the Palisades was a favorite spot of theirs—or by himself. He often spent Sundays sketching his way down the spine of Manhattan, starting at Spuyten Duyvil and working his way down to the Battery.

Price was born in 1901 and grew up in a tiny New Jersey hamlet called Coytesville, a community of four hundred souls, many of whom seemed to have turned up in Price's later drawings. After graduating from high school, George landed his first job with the telephone company, which was beginning to install the latest dial technology. For this he received seventeen cents an hour. Eventually George found a job with a small ad agency, and worked there long enough to save passage for himself to and from Europe. In 1927 he took the obligatory trip to Paris. (He was there when Lindy landed.) "Pop" Hart's studio was a kind of gathering spot for the artists of the day, and George met, along with the cartoonists R. Dirkes and George Herriman, the Mexican muralist Diego Rivera. Hart was a sophisticated painter and passionately in touch with the avant-garde. As a result, when Price arrived in Paris he was well prepared to seek out and enjoy the best art of his time. His lifelong addiction to collecting was already manifesting itself, and he returned with drawings and prints by, among others, Klee and Picasso, which still hang proudly on the walls of his eighteenth-century Dutch farmhouse in New Jersey. Over the years George's collecting interests ranged widely. The house is stunningly furnished with seventeenth- and eighteenth-century antiques, and contains one of the finest collections of antique American glass still in private hands. When George returned to the states, he began selling sketches and accepting assignments from magazines as diverse as *Collier's*, *Life*, *Judge*, and eventually *The New Yorker*. After purchasing a few spots from Price, Katharine White invited

Bird's Eye Maple late Rutherford B. Hayes — Not a Collector's Item but lots of fun.

Victorian Chaise-Lounge Comfortable if you're round-shouldered. They don't bring much.

Gas Meter Courtesy of Public Service Corp. of N.J.

Occasional Table Top and Bottom are Restorations.

Palisades Interstate Park — where who meets whom and other relatives.

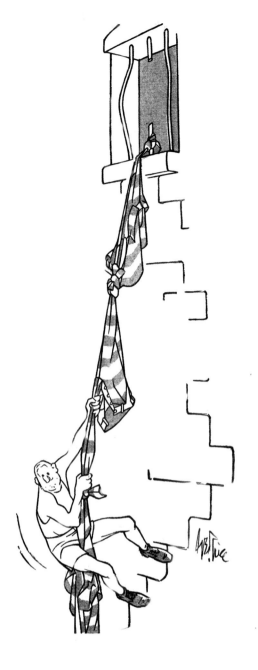

him in for an interview. She encouraged him to try his hand at cartooning. George was reluctant at first. He was not an idea person. Mrs. White promised to supply him with gag writers, and on this condition George was persuaded to begin submitting to the magazine. Over his long and prolific career George produced only one idea of his own—the wonderful cover drawing of a gaggle of Santa Clauses in a subway car.

That an artist as idiosyncratic as George Price could be completely dependent on idea men may seem at first to defy common sense. In fact, once George had established his essential cast of characters, his dysfunctional extended family, creating ideas for him was somewhat like writing for a well-cast sitcom. And like the best comedians, George could often interpret even a weak idea so that it seemed inspired. George's repertory of crackpots and misfits may seem to be merely the product of a brilliant imagination, but in fact, with the possible exception of the sideshow freaks and the man floating above the bed featured in his early work, most of his human menagerie were drawn from his neighbors in Coytesville. It was farm

country and the population was mostly German and Irish. As George described them, they seem to have been a remarkable group. There were the brothers Picky, Motsy, Rotsy, and Nuthin, who hung out at Gus Becker's saloon. What they had in common were heads the size and shape of grapefruits. There was also the eccentric down the road who moved fence posts around in the middle of the night, slowly slicing off bits of her neighbor's property. And there was the neighbor who stole the church steeple and added it to his own house.

In light of the dazzling virtuosity of George's draftsmanship, it is easy to overlook the solid architecture that underlies his compositions. His preliminary sketches, usually produced in pencil on tracing paper, make it clear that even the simplest drawings have been composed and recomposed with an eye not only to clarity but to establishing that rhythm and flow which characterize his work. George's taste for the grotesque extended, of course, beyond the characters in his drawings to the world they inhabit. The bastard furniture he specialized in has its own charm, and who else could make

"Whew! 'Tain't a fit night out for man nor beast!"

the back of a television set look interesting?

George was a harsh critic of other people's work and was seldom satisfied with his own. However, on one occasion, when James Geraghty expressed admiration for a Price drawing of a plumber working in a flooded basement in an inflatable swan, George did admit he felt that no steamfitter could find any problem with the way he had drawn the plumbing.

Most artists are angry people, but George was a passionate hater. The depth of his loathing for professional saints, bleeding hearts, advertising men, professional do-gooders, self-improvement freaks, and politicians of all persuasions has never been adequately expressed in his cartoons. Over the years he produced a memorable gallery of these grotesques, most of them too brutally honest to be presented in a family periodical. Whereas in his cartoons line seems to leap and dance, here it cuts like a whip. The bitter brilliance of these drawings was well captured in a collection published several years ago called *Ice Cold War*. Three of these drawings are reproduced on this page. Unforgiving caricatures of

public figures as diverse as J. Edgar Hoover and Elsa Maxwell are flayed and mounted over snippets from Shakespeare. The result is a rogues' gallery of the pompous, foolish, and venal. Comparing these drawings with George's cartoons, one is forced to acknowledge the restraining effect of the *New Yorker*'s gag writers on his wit. I'm not sure this was a bad thing. George's various collaborators encouraged a more forgiving view of humanity than one finds in these masterful but chilling sketches.

Although George had a dour view of mankind, it was combined with a strong sense of personal honor. For most of the years I worked with him, his ideas were supplied by one gentleman, a sometime cartoonist named John Corcoran. The magazine paid Corcoran for the ideas George used, but George took it upon himself to share with John any subsequent royalties generated from either reprints or anthology use.

George stopped drawing for publication in 1990, but he continued to sketch into his ninety-third year. We hope that one day these final drawings, whether bitter or sweet, will be collected and available for the enjoyment of his large and loyal public.

"Ram thou thy fruitful tidings in mine ears, . . ."
ANTONY AND CLEOPATRA

"He'll tickle it for his concupy."
TROILUS AND CRESSIDA

"Call all your tribes together, praise the gods, And make triumphant fires. . . ."
CORIOLANUS

A NAZI HISTORY OF THE WORLD
Richard Coeur de Lion Shares the Rough Camp Fare with His Followers

"We have no regular art staff." This quote is from a letter from Katharine White to a job seeker and the letter is dated March 25, 1930. By 1939, when James Geraghty was invited to join the magazine as "head of the art department," *The New Yorker* was widely celebrated for its cartoons, its covers, and the clean, classic layout of its pages. Amazingly, all this had been accomplished without either an art editor in the usual sense or the support of anything one could reasonably call an art department. Tuesday art meetings were still being chaired by Ross and attended by Irvin. But the responsibility for dealing with the artists was rotated among various staff members, including Scudder Middleton, Wolcott Gibbs, Katharine White, and William Maxwell. (Philip Wylie had left the magazine in 1928.) Gibbs and the writer Russell Maloney were also responsible for looking through the so-called slush pile (the week's collection of unsolicited cartoons). All of these people had other, more demanding editorial responsibilities. The one constant in this shifting mix was Daise Terry, Ross's former secretary, who took notes at the art meeting and oversaw the assignment of art and the distribution of OKs.

The so-called make-up department was equally fragmented. Carmine Peppe and his small staff—Joe Carroll and Frank Grisaitis—assembled each week's issue, vetted the final proofs, and dispatched the magazine to the printers. Another group, led by Howard Knowles, laid out the front of the book and selected the cartoons for each week's issue. The covers were proofed in the business department. With the exception of Rea Irvin, who was at the magazine only two days a week, none of these people had any background in either creating art or preparing it for reproduction. The truth is that Ross, who cried for order the way Macbeth cried for light, had never bothered to create a single department to handle one of the glories of *The New Yorker*, its art. The magazine, to deal with Ross's oversight, seems to have solved the problem by itself. The "art department" was not an entity but a process shaped in Darwinian fashion by the constant pressures of weekly deadlines. In 1939 the *New Yorker*'s art department was a triumph of evolutionary bricolage. Perhaps Ross sensed that continuing to depend on such a fragile system was tempting fate. Or perhaps the magazine just wanted to have James Geraghty's considerable gag-writing skills closer to hand.

In any case, in the fall of 1939 James Geraghty was invited by William Maxwell to take charge of the art department. James Geraghty had first made himself known to the magazine the previous year as a writer of gag ideas. Like Ross, Thurber, and many other *New Yorker* people, Geraghty

James Geraghty

August 12, 1940

Mr. Shuman:

Mr. Geraghty has agreed to go through the Art Bank, and more important from my standpoint, bring up any pictures he thinks are duds and ought to be killed. I think it is very important that this be done periodically and a check made on drawings held up for some time. It is like Newsbreaks, stuff stagnating and stalling, and me with no confidence. I damn near fell off the chair today when I saw the attached drawing in the issue. It is a little thing several years old that Weekes and Knowles put in when the snow came. It would have been fine when bought and jokes of the depression were having a run. Now I am quite certain it won't mean a damn thing to the reader. It will just throw him for a loop.

Geraghty (who says he wants to work further into the Art) has also agreed to wise himself up on the cover situation so he will know in Art Meeting what our needs are, what we have against these needs, and what to have in prospect against them, etc. I am getting frantic not knowing where we stand on covers and want the responsibility on one person and I think I have got it there by this move.

H. W. Ross

cc: Mr. Geraghty
   Mr. Lobrano

was from the West. His résumé included early work in the lead mines of Idaho, driving a truck in Seattle, working as a bookkeeper in New York at McGraw-Hill and, most recently, in the late thirties, trying his hand as a writer of comedy for radio. His ambition in this area was waning as a result of slow pay and the constant calls for rewrites. In a magazine called *The Writer* he read that many cartoonists used gag ideas. Geraghty, who was familiar with *The New Yorker*, looked through a few issues and jotted down names of the cartoonists. These he checked against the Manhattan phone book. When he had a list of a dozen or so, he sat down at his typewriter and dashed off a few pages of ideas. His first mailings led to sales to artists such as Perry Barlow, Richard Decker, Barney Tobey, and, most importantly, Peter Arno. A correspondence developed between Arno and Geraghty over the question of payments and eventually led Geraghty to an interview at the magazine with William Maxwell, the fiction editor who often dealt with problems involving the artists. In this case the problem was the failure of Arno to pay for ideas that Geraghty had submitted, Arno had drawn, and the magazine had published. Arno was proficient in many areas, but he had a lifelong difficulty in signing his name to a check. Eventually *The New Yorker* picked up the tab: fifty dollars a piece.

Encouraged by his early success, Geraghty, as he recalls in notes for an unpublished book on his years at *The New Yorker*, allowed his imagination to run wild. He had fantasies of becoming a gentleman farmer in New Hampshire, supporting himself with weekly sales to *The New Yorker* and *New Yorker* contributors. I think even Jim was surprised at how quickly he tossed this dream out the window when William Maxwell asked him to accept a job at the magazine. Maxwell believes that Geraghty was hired with the limited responsibility of replacing him as liaison between the art meeting and the artists. This meant, in addition to attending the Tuesday art meetings, meeting each Thursday with an eager group of non-staff artists from whom the magazine plucked occasional ideas for its regular contributors. From the beginning, however, Geraghty made it clear that he felt his mandate was considerably broader. Halfway through his first day on the job he informed Maxwell, who was hanging around to show Jim the ropes, that he no longer needed his assistance. Typical of Ross's *New Yorker*, the job came with no job description. In fact, according to Geraghty, although he was the de facto art editor from 1939 on, it was only during the war, under pressure from the government to provide job descriptions for all employees, that Geraghty finally became art editor de jure. (Irvin was then described as art director.) Geraghty's first art meeting, the first of sixteen hundred, was in September of '39. In attendance were Ross, Rea Irvin, of course, Gus Lobrano from the fiction department, and Daise Terry. There was also a young man who acted as art boy and presented the drawings on a small easel for the rest of the staff to consider. The art boy at that meeting was the very young and very bored Truman Capote. The meeting was held in a small conference room next to Ross's office which was used for no other purpose. Daise Terry distributed knitting needles to serve as pointers. Irvin's thoughts on this occasion have not been recorded. Although some writers have suggested that toward the end of his life Irvin expressed some bitterness toward the magazine, it seems to have been more a question of rejected drawings than the sudden appearance of James Geraghty.

The other person at the art meetings who had reason to be disturbed by Geraghty's presence was Daise Terry. Miss Terry, as she was called, was a strong-willed, sharp-tongued woman. She considered herself a member of the *New Yorker* A-team, a position she jealously guarded. She kept the minutes of the art meetings and typed up comments to be passed along to the artists. Gus Lobrano and William Maxwell were called in occasionally when artists required "special handling," but distributing OKs, keeping the records, and logging in the finishes was Miss Terry's province. Ross, who didn't mind stirring things up a bit, further complicated the situation by making Miss Terry Geraghty's secretary. Jim reports that after introducing the two of them—that is, Terry and Geraghty—Ross threw his hands in the air, turned his back, and said, "And may the best man win." This is a good story, although "best" seems unlikely, coming as it does from the man whose bedside reading was Fowler's *Dictionary of Modern English Usage.*

The drawings on these pages were a gift to William Maxwell from one of the Thursday group of hopefuls.

June 24, 1946

Mr. Truax:

Mr. Geraghty says that the artists do not realize how much they are being paid per picture, since some of their earnings go to them indirectly. He says artists are always surprised when he tells them the prices they are averaging. I recommend that some routine way of reminding them of their per picture earnings be worked out. For instance, we might get up and distribute to them every so often—say every six months—an analysis of earnings that would have this average price in it. It seems to me it would be a good psychology to do something like this.

H. W. Ross

cc: Mr. Geraghty
Mr. Mason

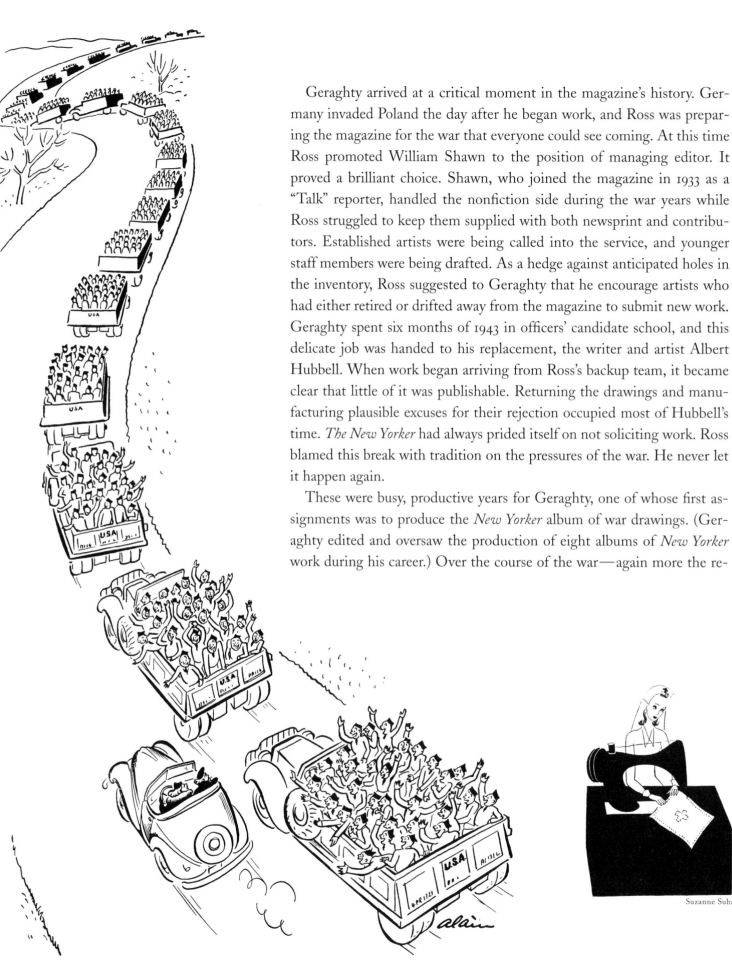

Geraghty arrived at a critical moment in the magazine's history. Germany invaded Poland the day after he began work, and Ross was preparing the magazine for the war that everyone could see coming. At this time Ross promoted William Shawn to the position of managing editor. It proved a brilliant choice. Shawn, who joined the magazine in 1933 as a "Talk" reporter, handled the nonfiction side during the war years while Ross struggled to keep them supplied with both newsprint and contributors. Established artists were being called into the service, and younger staff members were being drafted. As a hedge against anticipated holes in the inventory, Ross suggested to Geraghty that he encourage artists who had either retired or drifted away from the magazine to submit new work. Geraghty spent six months of 1943 in officers' candidate school, and this delicate job was handed to his replacement, the writer and artist Albert Hubbell. When work began arriving from Ross's backup team, it became clear that little of it was publishable. Returning the drawings and manufacturing plausible excuses for their rejection occupied most of Hubbell's time. *The New Yorker* had always prided itself on not soliciting work. Ross blamed this break with tradition on the pressures of the war. He never let it happen again.

These were busy, productive years for Geraghty, one of whose first assignments was to produce the *New Yorker* album of war drawings. (Geraghty edited and oversaw the production of eight albums of *New Yorker* work during his career.) Over the course of the war—again more the re-

Suzanne Suba

"The best thing to do is just pay no attention."

sult of attrition than design—a true art department began to take shape. Howard Knowles did not return, and his responsibilities were shifted to Carmine Peppe's make-up department. Geraghty was now the single person dealing with the artists. Jim had no art background but had a wonderful eye and seems to have known instinctively how to get from each artist his or her best work.

His strong suit, of course, was as a writer, and he kept every Thursday free to work on developing ideas and fine-tuning captions. Jim has left us his own thoughts on these quiet afternoons in his smoke-filled office. They curiously echo Ross's editorial guidelines, and perhaps explain why the two worked together so well. About his work Jim wrote: "I felt a caption had to scan, this word first, then that word, not the other way. No conscious alliteration. No poetic contrivance." Ross would have applauded these thoughts. Some years after Jim first came to the magazine, he asked William Maxwell why he had hired him in the first place. Maxwell replied, "Because you looked like a gentleman and I wanted to leave." That is, leave to devote more time to his own writing. This response to me seems somewhat ingenuous. It was Jim's skill as a writer and editor of humor that Ross

The relationship between De Vries and Geraghty was a fruitful one for both the cartoonists and the magazine. De Vries's comic novels were becoming increasingly successful, and his 1954 best-seller, called *The Tunnel of Love*, was inspired to a large extent by his experiences in the magazine's art department. Geraghty found the book amusing and congratulated De Vries on his success. He thought no more about it, until he realized that some people believed the protagonist, a philandering art editor at a sophisticated magazine, was a portrait of him. De Vries denied any such intent, and in the stage version undercut that interpretation by having *The New Yorker* mentioned as a competing magazine, thus establishing it and Jim as separate from his imaginary weekly.

was after. But of course he could not have known what a fine editor of the magazine's art Geraghty would become.

As Jim expanded the reach of the art department during the war, he was fortunate to receive some crackerjack assistance. Like William Maxwell, Peter De Vries was an editor who was looking to reduce his responsibilities. He had been editing poetry ever since Ross had lured him away from *Poetry* magazine in 1942.

Peter was developing a reputation as a comic writer and wanted to spend more time on his own work. With Geraghty's encouragement he resigned as *Poetry* editor and accepted a position as a part-time editor and sometime creator of cartoon captions. Although this responsibility brought him into the office only one day a week, De Vries took it very seriously, as the example of his caption editing on page 107 suggests.

At this time Jim was seeing regular contributors every Tuesday and occasionally meeting with promising new talent on Wednesday. Like Rea Irvin he was reluctant to deliver the bad news involved in such a process. To handle this and several other unpleasant chores, Jim hired on a part-time basis a young cartoonist from Philadelphia whose work was just beginning to appear in the magazine, Frank Modell. Frank continued this job till Jim retired and, with little recognition, helped break in a whole new generation of artists.

Under Geraghty, the art department was becoming the one department that handled all aspects of the art of the magazine. By the fifties he was scheduling covers, overseeing the editing of captions, buying spots, and meeting regularly with the artists and make-up department. Rea Irvin continued to sit in on the art meetings, but Geraghty was clearly at that point the art editor. After Ross's death in '51, Rea Irvin drifted away from the magazine. Outwardly, he remained as gracious and dignified in his retirement years as he had been during the magazine's tumultuous early days. Had he written his own story of *The New Yorker*, our picture of the magazine might be somewhat different. From what we do know, however, his central importance in creating the graphic armature for Ross's vision remains unchallenged. Without Rea Irvin as midwife, the *New Yorker*'s style would never have been born.

The war did bring one remarkable new artist to the magazine. Charlie Addams was stationed in Astoria, Queens, in a division of the signal corps that produced training films. Several members of the staff were from the Disney Studios. Addams encouraged one particularly gifted young man named Sam Cobean to bring some of his sketches to *The New Yorker*, where they caused a sensation. Though his career was short—he died in a car crash in 1951—his work had a powerful impact on his contemporaries. Dana Fradon, Robert Kraus, Bernard Wiseman, Frank Modell, and even Charles Addams himself were influenced by him. Saul Steinberg edited a posthumous collection of his drawings, which included an introduction and a tribute by Addams.

"But we're from 'Life'!"

"*Well, you can go right back to Dr. Richard T. Robbins and tell him I said your trouble is not psychiatric.*"

cobean

cobean

"If you'll excuse me, Madam, I should like to make a purchase."

"I'd think you would have learned by now that seniority doesn't count for a thing around here."

Bill Fitzgerald, Bernie McAteer, Joe Carroll, and Carmine Peppe (far right) in the layout department on Forty-third Street

By this time, *The New Yorker*'s basic format was well established. The magazine opened with "Goings On," then proceeded to "Notes and Comment" and "The Talk of the Town." Profiles, fiction, and reportage followed. There were casuals, poetry, criticism. Theatre was invariably illustrated with a caricature by Al Frueh. "Talk," of course, featured the drawings of Otto Soglow. There were spots throughout, but the only visual feature to compete with the magazine's advertisers was the cartoons. The number varied from week to week, usually ranging from fifteen to twenty, depending on the heft of the issue. In these early issues, cartoons appear almost as footprints, upper left, lower right, upper right, lower left—moving leisurely down the highway of text. The responsibility for assembling these ingredients into a package suitable for publication was divided between the layout department and the make-up department. The make-up department was presided over by the volcanic Carmine Peppe, who had joined the staff in 1925. His earliest responsibilities were as a kind of office boy and included everything from sharpening pencils to providing the black coffee that revived the staff after the long, alcoholic lunches that were common at that time. Though untrained, Carmine had a sharp eye and also a low threshold for pretension. These two attributes stood him in good stead over the years. Carmine was short, quick-tempered, and Italian. Everyone else in the make-up department seemed to be large, easygoing, and Irish.

The make-up department was a hot, dingy, high-ceilinged space whose dirty windows and cracked paint called to mind a police station in the outer boroughs. Copy sheets, trimmed with twelve-inch shears, were secured to dummy pages with straight pins. The dummy pages were hung on walls, and the small staff struggled across floors littered with discarded proofs, layouts, and cigarette butts.

Peppe worked the staff hard, but no harder than himself. Lunch was regularly eaten standing at the worktables, and late deadlines often required sleepovers. This atmosphere of controlled chaos, often reminiscent of a Marx Brothers movie, seemed to be irresistible to writers and artists on the staff. They often dropped by to chat and offer suggestions. Carmine seldom had time to chat and he did not welcome suggestions. On Thursdays, as the final closing approached, the air was thick with curses and cigarette smoke.

Today there are no straight pins, no shears, some cursing, but definitely no smoking! Each week's issue is assembled by a small team under the leadership of Pat Keogh and Mike Bullerdick. They work their magic in a large well-lit space filled with the latest computer technology. Although satisfying the competing demands of writers, artists, and editors and still meeting inexorable deadlines keeps the emotional temperature high, the room is pleasantly air-conditioned all year round.

Joe Carroll, who ran the art department from Peppe's retirement in 1975 to his own in 1985, looks back on those early years affectionately. "We worked hard," he said, "but we had fun." One of Joe's favorite stories involved a casual by Eugene Kinkead about an eccentric Manhattanite known as the Cat Lady. This woman spent her days collecting homeless cats, dropping them in a burlap bag, and delivering them to the ASPCA, where she hoped they would find a better fate. In Kinkead's piece she is described as "fortyish." "Eccentric" she may have been, but as a woman she took exception to "fortyish." She appeared at the outer office of *The New Yorker* one afternoon and demanded to see Kinkead. When she learned that he was not on the premises, she unloaded her day's haul of stray cats on the receptionist's desk. Dozens of cats, hungry and terrified, disappeared into various offices, both empty and occupied, on the seventeenth floor. It took a week to find and remove them all.

Mike Bullerdick and Janet Riley consult with Haig Sarajian of Quality House of Graphics while Pat Keogh mans the computer.

Harold Ross had a horror of life's "big questions," and firmly believed that dwelling on them could only lead to madness and suicide. Ross's attitude is reflected in the early magazine. His contributors were encouraged to think locally and write short. There is an inverse snobbery in this attitude, and *The New Yorker* in the years prior to the Second World War was often guilty of a kind of self-congratulatory indifference to the larger issues. For example, in the anniversary issue of 1930, a note in "The Talk of the Town" proudly announced that in its five years of publication the magazine had successfully crusaded for only two issues, one of which was moving the information booth at Penn Station from the side wall to the center of the main concourse. The Second World War changed all that. The brilliant reportage of the war years set new standards for the magazine's journalists, and writers no longer felt uncomfortable writing about serious issues seriously. The long reflective pieces, from John Hersey's "Hiroshima" to James Baldwin's "The Fire Next Time," fit comfortably into

Main Street

"Au secours! Sauvez-moi! Au secours!"

"If he's not a Frenchman, he's certainly an awful snob."

the postwar magazine in a way that would have been impossible before the forties. One can hardly imagine, for example, Peter Arno saying, "Drawing is a way of reasoning on paper."

This is a 1978 quote from the Steinberg we all recognize, the one who was being celebrated in a sprawling retrospective at the Whitney Museum of American Art. There was an earlier Steinberg, who made his first appearance in the magazine as a graphic journalist in 1940, sending in sketches of adventures in India, China, and the Far East as an interpreter with the OSS under the celebrated "Wild Bill" Donovan. We know now that this Steinberg was a kind of disguise behind which there lay Steinberg the metaphysician, Steinberg a "writer of pictures, an architect of speech and sounds, a draftsman of philosophical reflections," as Harold Rosenberg described him. This Steinberg revealed himself not in the reportage of the forties but in the covers and spreads that began to appear with increasing frequency in the magazine in the fifties.

Air raid

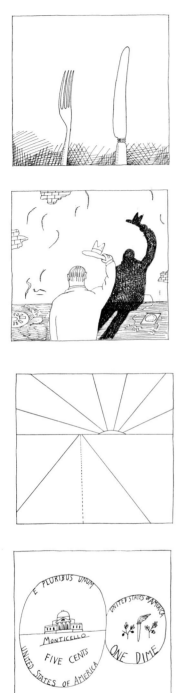

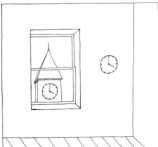

Saul Steinberg was born in Romania in 1914. His father had a small print shop and also manufactured containers of all kinds. As a young man Saul studied architecture in Milan, an experience that prepared him not for architecture but for his later career as a graphic artist. He was awarded a doctorate in architecture in 1940. His diploma seems to have been the inspiration for later reflections on authenticity. It was awarded "To Saul Steinberg, of the Jewish race," and signed by Victor Emmanuel III, king of Italy, king of Albania, emperor of Ethiopia. Steinberg says, "It was some kind of safeguard for the future, meaning that although I was a doctor, I could be boycotted from practicing, since I am a Jew. The beauty for me is that this diploma was given by the king but he is no longer king of Italy. He is no more king of Albania. He is not even the emperor of Ethiopia, and I am not an architect. The only thing that remains is 'razza Ebraica,' ('of the Jewish race')."

His career as a cartoonist began while he was still in architecture school in Milan selling drawings to the satirical publication *Bertoldo*. It is important to note that Saul has always insisted that his goal is the published work, not the artifact on the gallery wall. His drawings, as separate from his constructions, are produced to be reproduced, and he has always insisted that we at *The New Yorker* not remove erasures, crop marks, or other signs of the process

of reproduction in the plates of his work. Saul has always had an interest in, even an affection for, the hardworking professionals in the magazine's make-up department. He usually schedules his appointments with the editors so that they leave him time to discuss fine points of reproduction with Carmine Peppe and his successors, and when a cover is being scheduled, he is constantly on the phone monitoring its progress. Indeed, the progressive sheets that are received from the color separator are often passed along to Saul himself for his approval.

In the 1940s, life as a Jew in Italy was becoming increasingly uncomfortable, and Saul left for Portugal. From there, after a detour to Santo Domingo, he arrived in the United States, under the sponsorship of *The New Yorker,* in 1942. The bus trip from his port of disembarkation, Miami, to New York was just the first of many expeditions around the country. Saul loves to travel and has visited all of the fifty states. From these travels he has developed his unique vocabulary, a highly personal syntax based on his views, real and

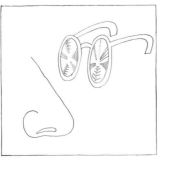

Over the years Saul has developed and refined this graphic vocabulary, but the core images of Uncle Sam, Mickey Mouse, and the Chrysler Building persist. There's an interesting parallel to the work of Price, Steig, Hokinson, Arno, and later George Booth and Roz Chast, all of whom also developed basic stock companies from which they continually cast their work. This private vocabulary has been widely copied, and, in Saul's eyes, to some extent devalued. The *New Yorker*'s inability to prevent this from happening has occasionally strained his relationship with the magazine. The most famous and painful example, of course, is Saul's cover of the world as perceived by the average New Yorker.

CHRYSLER BUILDING AT 42ND STREET

imaginary, of the American experience. Uncle Sam, Mickey Mouse, majorettes, corporate automatons, Santa Claus, the Easter Bunny, and later, darker visions of city life—crocodiles that roam the streets like homeless dogs, police cars lit up like airports, street punks, whores, and his favorite ideogram for America's marriage of art and commerce, the Chrysler Building. Baseball, which Saul considers a key to understanding America, also figures prominently in both his drawings and his conversation.

In Jim Geraghty's notes on his years with the magazine, the ambivalence of his relationship with William Shawn is apparent. He clearly admired both Shawn and Ross. It is equally clear that Jim had a kind of rough-and-tumble relationship with Ross which he found congenial, and that Shawn's more formal manner made him uncomfortable. There was also a difference in artistic sensibility which really didn't make itself known until after Jim retired. Conversations with Frank Modell and others suggest that Jim expected to run the art department independently after Ross's death, and that the depth of Shawn's involvement—he insisted on being a part of every level of the decision-making process—surprised him. Within one month of becoming editor, he reassigned the art boy, "excused" Gus Lobrano from the art meetings, and encouraged Rea Irvin to retire. In fact, though he often deferred to Geraghty (for example, in Jim's reluctance to approach Jules Feiffer), Shawn quickly made it clear that he had his own strong ideas about the magazine's art. It was Shawn, not Geraghty, as has been widely supposed, who was responsible for phasing out the magazine's reliance on gagmen. Shawn felt strongly that *The New Yorker* should publish artists who created their own ideas, and this gave a new generation of artists that included Ed Koren, George Booth, Warren Miller, Jim Stevenson, Don Reilly, Bud Handelsman, Charlie Barsotti, and myself the opportunity to appear in the magazine more frequently than we might otherwise have, had our ideas still been regularly farmed out to more established contributors.

Shawn's own taste, which ran to the delicate and subdued, was not noticeably reflected on the covers during the fifties and sixties. However, during this period Shawn was commissioning sketches and illustrations for the fact pieces directly through his office, and it is in these that we first get a glimpse of the changes that would be evident in the magazine's art after Geraghty's departure.

Huntley and Brinkley

Marvin Minsky

Julia Child

Tony Bennett

A rough drawing is the artist's first draft of his or her idea. It needn't be polished, but it should clearly depict all important aspects of the setting and give a good sense of the characters. These are usually drawn on 8½-by-11-inch sheets of typewriter paper, although many artists work larger. Everett Opie, for example, produced poster-size roughs 24 by 32 inches. Some, for practical reasons, work smaller. Charlie Barsotti's sketches, which he mails in from Kansas City, are barely larger than index cards. At the bottom of each drawing, the artist types or writes—legibly, one hopes—the caption. The artist's name and address should be on the back of each piece.

Most cartoonists produce between fifteen and thirty idea sketches per week. The artists who use written gags translate them to this rough form before submitting them to the magazine.

There are as many techniques for coming up with ideas as there are cartoonists. Henry Martin puts a blank piece of paper on his drawing table and keeps staring at it until he comes up with an idea. He then pencils it in, types on the caption, and puts a fresh piece of paper in front of himself. Many artists prime the pump by browsing through news magazines or *The New York Times*. It's not considered unsporting to flip through back issues of *The New Yorker* itself. Although a few blessed souls seem to be able to pluck ideas out of the blue, for most cartoonists the creation of ideas is the most difficult part of the workweek.

If you've been keeping track of the figures mentioned above—that is, fifteen to thirty drawings a week per artist, times forty artists under contract, plus the hundreds of unsolicited weekly submissions—you begin to get some idea of the quixotic nature of the cartoonist's enterprise.

Part of the art editor's job is to

In the spring of 1950 I graduated from high school, and in that fall, I entered what was called the Foundation Art Program at Carnegie Institute, now Carnegie Mellon, in Pittsburgh. In high school an extraordinary teacher, the only person I ever knew who could cut a mat freehand, had introduced me to the paintings of Arshile Gorky, Jackson Pollock, and the Abstract Expressionists. It was their star I was determined to follow. This ambition was sharpened after I transferred to Pratt Institute and studied painting and drawing with Philip Guston.

By 1956, two years after graduation, my modest success was insufficient to support myself and a growing family. The father of a high school friend who had been impressed with sketches I had done for the high school yearbook (very much in a "Steinbergian" mode) suggested I try cartooning. The name of this kind and generous man was Jack Morley. Jack was a cartoonist himself and knew the field well. He had worked with Fontaine Fox on "Toonerville Folks" and was Crockett Johnson's assistant on the seminal strip "Barnaby." (Barnaby was a small boy, and his adventures with his imaginary fairy grandfather served as the prototype of today's successful "Calvin and Hobbes.")

My only regular source of income at that time came from playing jazz cornet with a band of recent Yale graduates, so I was willing to try anything. With Jack's advice and encouragement, I sketched up a group of rough ideas, and armed with a cartoon market guide from the *Writer's Digest*, I began to make the weekly rounds.

The cartoon marketplace was both broader and deeper in those days, and a fledgling talent, even with my limited experience, could manage with persistence to get his work published somewhere. In addition to *The New Yorker*, *The Saturday Evening Post*, *Look*, *Collier's*, *Sports Illustrated*, and *This Week*, a weekly newspaper supplement, all published general-interest cartoons. *Esquire* featured full-color work, as did the spectacularly successful *Playboy* and its dozens of imitators. There were also the men's magazines—adventure- and sports-oriented, such as *True*, *Cavalier*, and the products of a group called Magazine Management. (Magazine Management was famous for its sensational, if unverifiable, stories such as "I Was Mussolini's Mistress.") As well as being a major cartoon market, Magazine Management provided support for a whole generation of struggling young writers, including Joseph Heller, James Lincoln Collier, Bruce Jay Friedman, and Mario Puzo.

The cartoonist's week in those days began on Thursday, when he sat down to work on ideas, and ended the following Wednesday, when most of the magazines that published cartoons offered an opportunity to submit work directly to the cartoon editor.

With the week's roughs under his arm, the artist would start the rounds at the top of the list, *The Saturday Evening Post*. (*The New Yorker*, at that time, saw only regular contributors. Unsolicited work had to be dropped off.) The *Post* was first choice because it bought the most, paid the most, and because coffee and jelly donuts were often available.

Out of the batch of twenty or so, the *Post* editor, John Bailey, might hold three for further consideration. Work from the previous week that had been OK'd for finish would be presented to the artist at this time, along with any editorial suggestions regarding either the caption or the drawing itself. The artist would then add to his remaining batch of seventeen the rejects he had collected from the *Post* and move to the next market, where the process would be repeated. By the end of a good Wednesday, a cartoonist would have collected several OKs and, more importantly, be sure his work would be represented at upcoming art meetings at over a dozen magazines.

Most magazines had an editor looking at material on Wednesday, and the day's rounds usually ended up at Dell Publications' magazine, *1000 Jokes*. *1000 Jokes* published puzzles, humorous verse, short humor, and dozens and dozens of cartoons. The editors themselves were usually in the field. Bill Yates and John Norment were two generous editors I particularly recall. Very few cartoonists were turned away with fewer than two or three OKs.

In retrospect, those were golden years. Beginning cartoonists had the opportunity to see their work in print, make a modest living, and at the same time develop a style. The situation was something analogous to a comedian polishing his act in the Catskills. By the end of the sixties, however, television had destroyed most of the general-interest mass-circulation markets, and cartoonists were struggling to survive in a rapidly shrinking marketplace.

screen all this material, approximately three thousand drawings a week, and winnow it down to a size one person can carry to the art meeting. The muse seems to ebb and flow, although not with the phases of the moon, so the number of drawings deemed suitable for the editors' consideration is not constant. It did not surprise me to learn that Jim Geraghty brought to his art meetings with Ross roughly what I brought to my art meetings with Shawn, Robert Gottlieb, and Tina Brown—that is, anything from forty-five to sixty sketches. Usually half of this group is OK'd and returned to the artist for finishing. Occasionally, rough sketches are deemed suitable for printing as is, but this is rare. Often some part of the sketch—an expression, a bit of body language, or just an elegantly laid wash—seems too good to cast aside and is incorporated by the artist into the finished piece. Indeed, most *New Yorker* finishes, if carefully examined, show evidence of this cosmetic surgery. The most extreme example of the collage technique is found in the work of George Booth. A Booth finish is likely to include parts—a head, a cactus, a trombone—cannibalized, not only from the rough OK'd sketch but from earlier discarded drawings. George attaches these to his finished drawings with teeny pieces of Scotch tape. The scars of this procedure are hidden from the general reader by the diligent efforts of our separators and the make-up department. The results are clearly visible, however, on the originals, and they give his work a rich tactile quality but also render them very vulnerable. Indeed, as George's drawings traveled around the country with *The New Yorker*'s sixtieth-anniversary show, it was occasionally necessary to remove them from their frames and reattach stray body parts that had worked loose in transit.

Although I experienced early success at *Look*, *Collier's*, *Esquire*, and other magazines, it soon became clear that a career could be built only at *The New Yorker*. At that time the magazine was still buying unsolicited roughs as well as written ideas and farming them out to regular contributors. Although I occasionally found encouraging notes from Jim Geraghty in my rejected batches, I submitted for over a year before he finally bought a rough of mine. It was drawn for the magazine by Richard Taylor. Over the next few months I sold several more, which were drawn by Addams, Darrow, and others. Finally, I was invited to try a finish myself. Frank Modell, the cartoonist and liaison between Jim Geraghty and prospective contributors, was not only talented but articulate, and he was a valuable tutor to beginning cartoonists such as myself. The possibility of actually appearing in *The New Yorker*, however, seemed to freeze whatever creative juices I had, and even with Frank's assistance I didn't seem to be able to complete a satisfactory finished drawing. Finally, in March of 1958, Geraghty himself invited me into his offices.

The New Yorker had been at 25 West Forty-third Street since the late twenties, and the space had been reshaped many times to accommodate the magazine's growth spurts. Offices had been enlarged or reconfigured as needed, and hardly a corridor existed that didn't include at least one false door. Jim's space had obviously been created out of two or possibly three small offices and had enough doors for a French farce. At the appointed hour, Don Hull, Jim's assistant, greeted me at the reception desk and escorted me back to the art department. Geraghty was an impressive figure; he was tall and slender, with arched brows that matched his silver hair. His complexion was pink and delicate, and he flushed easily as he spoke. His manner seemed both stern and bemused. After urging me to sit, he stood up, folded his arms (a characteristic gesture), and began pacing around the room. For some reason he seemed as ill at ease as I was and as he spoke he drifted out of his office into his secretary's adjoining office, then through the outer office, and finally back to where I sat. As a result, I was able to catch only bits and pieces of his remarks, but what I did hear astonished me. Jim Geraghty was offering me a contract with *The New Yorker* magazine. At the end of this extraordinary interview, he invited me to join the artists whom he met with personally every Wednesday. (There was also a Tuesday batch of more senior contributors.) He then handed me a large group of OKs he had saved from earlier submissions. Before I could recover from all this, Jim escorted me down to the

"Bon appétit!"

nineteenth floor and introduced me to the editor, William Shawn. Mr. Shawn seemed even more uncomfortable than Geraghty had been, but his words were gracious and encouraging. Although I often passed Mr. Shawn in the hallway over the next fifteen years, I don't believe we ever spoke again until he invited me to succeed Jim Geraghty as art editor in 1973.

By this time I had already met many *New Yorker* regulars, either in the magazine's outer office or more casually at the other magazines. (I recall first meeting Mischa Richter seated along with several other distinguished artists on a rolled-up carpet in the outer offices of *True* magazine. To be fair, the office was being painted, but this casual treatment of editorial talent was not exceptional.)

Don Reilly, Gahan Wilson, Robert Kraus, Joe Farris, and Chuck Saxon were familiar from the weekly rounds, as were Mort Walker (who later created "Beetle Bailey"), Johnny Hart (who went on to "B.C." and "The Wizard of Id"), and Charles Schulz, who was struggling to sell a strip about kids called "Lil' Folks." The Wednesday lunches often included some of the senior contributors such as Robert Day, Barney Tobey, and Whitney Darrow, Jr., as well as the gag writer Richard McCallister.

New Yorker readers seem to have firmly fixed ideas about the contributors to the magazine. Writers are considered to be monosyllabic, reclusive, and melancholic. Editors are considered to be either inspired amateurs on the model of Ross, I suppose, or donnish pedants—buttoned-down and bearded. The cartoonists are often thought to be a gaggle of irrepressible madcaps—stand-up comedians given to bathroom humor and practical jokes—W. C. Fields, the Marx Brothers, and the Algonquin Round Table all rolled into one. I must confess that to some extent I shared some of these preconceptions when I was first invited to join the Wednesday lunch group at one of its favorite spots, The Blue Ribbon.

The Blue Ribbon was a dark, dismal oak-paneled labyrinth on two floors of a slowly sinking building on West Forty-fourth Street. It was decorated with photos of forgotten opera stars and featured a staff of stiff-necked German waiters who were rumored to be survivors of Rommel's Afrika Korps. A setting less conducive to high jinks and hilarity would be hard to imagine. The service matched the atmosphere. When Dana Fradon once complained about the broken glass he found in his spinach, they simply brought him a fresh portion. Over the years the personnel at the luncheons has changed, but the rituals remain intact. After ordering drinks—martinis in those days, Perrier today—the conversation turns to what everyone had at the previous lunch. After you've lamented the missed opportunities made apparent by your neighbors' choices, the menus are distributed, and after further discussion everyone orders the same thing he had the last time. The funniest and truest line at these gatherings was Jim Geraghty's prayer, "Please, Lord, don't let me order the chicken club sandwich again." After orders are taken, the conversation turns to politics.

James Geraghty, gag writer Richard McCallister, me, and Charles Addams

There it remains until the last coffee cup is empty and the check arrives. While a few brave volunteers struggle to calculate and collect everyone's contribution, some comments on sports might be sprinkled on top of the conversation—a sprig of parsley on a great plate of hash.

With the passing years, the mood has lightened but the conversation still weighs a ton. Cartoonists are a solemn, if not lugubrious, lot. Laughter is their business, not their pastime, and when they gather, the humor tends to be dark. There are a few notable exceptions. Frank Modell is a delightful mimic and storyteller. Whitney Darrow's wit is as sharp as his pen. Arnold Roth has convulsed audiences both at lunch and on television. Charlie Addams could be quietly droll, and George Booth responds to his own remarks with such infectious laughter that it's impossible not to join in. For artist as entertainer, however, the all-time champ remains James Thurber. It may be that the lack of vivacity among today's cartoonists is less a constitutional failure than a reluctance to compete with the man who in 1933 had already established benchmark records for sharp repartee, inspired storytelling, and elaborate practical jokes. These have never been successfully challenged at *The New Yorker* or anywhere else.

Early in my *New Yorker* career, Jim Geraghty, in an expansive moment, offered me work space on the premises if I ever needed it. Since I was at that time happily married and living in Connecticut, it seemed like a safe offer. However, several years later, when I was unhappily unmarried and living back in New York, I took Jim up on his proposition. Space at the magazine being limited, I was shuttled daily from office to office as room became available from writers and editors when they went on vacation or left the premises for other, unexplained reasons.

My entire tool kit consisted of several pencils, an eraser, white-out, India ink, a brush to draw with, and one or two pads of drawing paper. So as not to disturb the desktop of my host or hostess, I learned to draw on a pad in my lap. I still do. (I discovered several years later that Rea Irvin, who could have had a studio the size of the Taj Mahal if he wished, worked in exactly the same way—at a small table halfway up the grand staircase in his elegant Connecticut home.) After a few months of this, and an ill-considered attempt to put me in a space carved out of the existing art department, I ended up in a small office at the far end of the eighteenth floor. My neighbors were Charles Addams and Warren Miller. Further down the hall were Frank Modell, Jim Stevenson, and Herbert Warren Wind, the sportswriter.

The New Yorker has always discouraged artists from nesting. To have a space was a great privilege and usually required wearing more than one hat. Frank Modell, of course, worked for Jim Geraghty; Jim Stevenson had started as a gag writer and continued to contribute written pieces as well as cartoons and covers. Warren Miller had been lured east from Chicago by the promise of an office. Charles Addams was—well—Charles Addams.

The exquisite etiquette of life at *The New Yorker* has been widely reported, and all the reports are true. Jim Stevenson once told me that during his high school summer internship at the magazine the only direction he received beyond his simple duties as office boy was to avoid at all costs speaking to Harold Ross. Since Jim had only a vague idea of what Ross looked like, he picked out the most formidable-looking person on the premises and spent the entire summer avoiding him. The figure turned out to be Rogers E. M. Whitaker, alias Colonel Frimbo, the railroad buff; Ross, who was ill at the time, rarely left his office.

The New Yorker is notorious for its insistence on the privacy of its artists and writers. Ross, being a practical man, believed that a necessary trip to the washroom should not break a creative person's train of thought. It should be an occasion not for social-

izing, but for quiet reflection. Casual conversation in the hallway or, worse, in the elevator was frowned upon, and an inquiry having to do with anyone's work in progress was unforgivable.

At that point in my life, a trip to the office was a ten-minute subway ride and then a three-block walk. My habit at the end of the day was to empty my keys, my subway tokens, and my small change into the cap I habitually wore. Arriving at the office one day, I removed my cap, hung up my jacket, and strolled down the hall to the men's room. No one I passed responded in any way to the fact, made clear to me as soon as I looked in the men's room mirror, that I had a dime in the middle of my forehead. Had I not gone to the men's room at that moment, I imagine I would have worn it till lunchtime.

The curious link between the *The New Yorker* and hot music was well established in the twenties. Peter Arno was a pianist and arranger, E. J. Kahn played saxophone, and legend has it that William Shawn once supported himself by playing stride piano in the bistros of Paris.

When I moved back to New York there was enough talent on the premises to form a kind of house band. Whitney Balliett on drums, staff reporter Wally White on piano, Paul Brodeur on clarinet, Warren Miller and Don Reilly on trumpets, and a friend of Warren's on bass. I was fortunate enough to have a large loft with a piano downtown, and this group and other friends, including occasionally Bill Steig's son Jeremy on flute, would be the core of weekly jam sessions. Sometimes we would move the group uptown to the town house of Daphne Hellman, Geoffrey Hellman's widow. Daphne played a hot harp, and her house always had some interesting musicians hanging around. During the sixties I can remember several sessions with a sitar player. This interest in jazz shared by Shawn and myself occasionally surfaced in cartoons and covers published in the magazine over our years together.

The freewheeling spirit of the sixties emerged in unexpected ways at *The New Yorker*. A group of young writers including Hendrik Hertzberg, George Trow, and Tony Hiss decided to create a communal work space out of their three contiguous offices. Crowbars and sledgehammers were obtained, and the project was launched with great enthusiasm—passersby were encouraged to join in. The picture of Penelope Gilliatt in high heels and a stylishly short skirt wielding a sledgehammer is still one of my most cherished memories from that period.

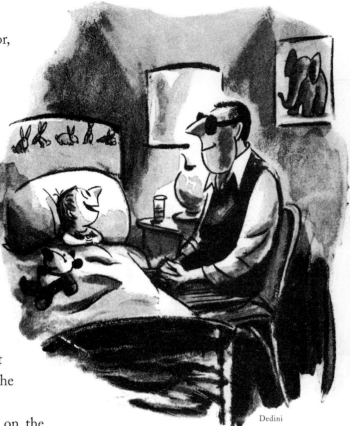

Dedini

"Pop, tell me again how jazz came up the river from New Orleans."

At *The New Yorker*, supplying the magazine with cartoons, covers, and spots was the art editor's second responsibility. The first one was supplying the magazine with artists. Since the twenties *The New Yorker* has sought out and developed artists who have been closely identified with the magazine.

The postwar years brought a fresh wave of cartoonists to the magazine, including Dana Fradon, Joe Mirachi, Robert Kraus, Eldon Dedini, Ed Fisher, Everett Opie, and Jim Mulligan. The late fifties and early sixties were an equally rich period. In the span of a few years Geraghty found such talents as Jim Stevenson, Bill Hamilton, Warren Miller, Bud Handelsman, Ed Koren, Robert Weber, Don Reilly, Charlie Barsotti, Joe Farris, and George Booth.

W Miller

Robert Weber

"I agree the book is definitely obscene, but do we want people to think we're square?"

"Aren't you being a little arrogant, son? Here's Lieutenant Colonel Farrington, Major Stark, Captain Truelove, Lieutenant Castle, and myself, all older and more experienced than you, and we think the war is _very_ moral."

"So much for kinetic art, eh, Leo?"

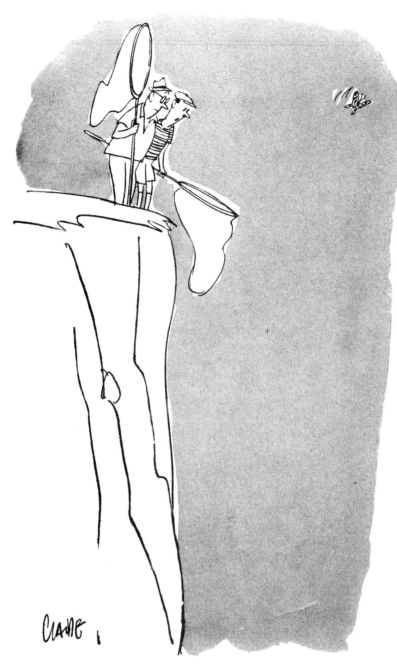

"He was a great lepidopterist."

"Look! Jim has the ball! See him run! Run, Jim, run!"

"We can be thankful we're not in the salad."

"Lucille, do we kiss the Friedlanders?"

Jim also introduced a remarkable late-bloomer named Charles Saxon. Chuck already had an established career in publishing as a writer and an executive when he decided to hang up his gray flannel suit and pursue his lifelong ambition to become a cartoonist. He and Geraghty were friends as well as neighbors, but when he told Jim of his decision, Geraghty was horrified. He spoke movingly of the vicissitudes of the cartoonist's life, but Chuck was determined. He had outlined a program for himself as a chronicler of the vacuity and despair at the core of affluent middle-class suburban life. Chuck was convinced that *The New Yorker* was the logical showcase for his enterprise, and, after resisting for over a year, Geraghty finally relented and began publishing what we can now recognize as one of the most significant bodies of social satire to come out in the last thirty years.

Chuck's skills as a draftsman were well matched by his talents as a writer, and some of his most notable pieces combine the two in unexpected new ways.

"If you're just going to brood, why not try your hand at some poetry?"

THE DAY THE TRAINS STOPPED

Ralph Miller, Ronald Smith, Gene Clifford, and Henry Thompson adjourned to the station luncheonette, where they played bridge until four o'clock in the afternoon.

Arthur Fenster was close to, but not actually a part of, a conversation between John Amster, Dick Burnside, Jr., and Tom Stanley, all golfers and members of the Chipowee Country Club. They were discussing their game. Fenster hoped they might start talking about the delay, so he could say something casual, like "You'd think they could make some sort of announcement. It wouldn't cost them anything."

Mrs. Lewis Fisher, member of the Republican Town Committee, said to her neighbor, Mrs. Lloyd Lefcourt, "There's more to this than meets the eye." Mrs. Lefcourt, who had matinée tickets to "The Sound of Music," said, "Be that as it may, discourtesy is certainly the order of the day."

At twelve o'clock noon, it became clear to Willis Palmer that the trains were not going to arrive. That, in fact, there never again would be an 8:47 to Grand Central. He thought of his family, in the neat board-and-batten split-level on the hill—of Francine, his wife; and Bill and Debby, his two young children. He knew he would have to give up his job in New York and try to find something in the country. Something close to home. Palmer folded his "Herald Tribune" neatly, dropped it in a litter basket, and walked slowly toward his Plymouth station wagon.

99

Since I first met James Geraghty in the late fifties, he had spoken often, if vaguely, of retiring. These remarks had become as familiar as his battles with Carmine Peppe, and when he announced in 1972 that he actually *was* retiring, we were all stunned.

Jim's decision may have been prompted by rumors of a mandatory retirement plan, or it may have been a result of his stated desire to spend more time reflecting, writing, and tending to his beloved roses. Whatever the reason, his scheduled departure caused great consternation among the artists, most of whom had never worked with another editor.

The question of Geraghty's successor was widely and sometimes heatedly discussed by the staff and among the artists. The consensus among the cartoonists and cover people was that the replacement should be drawn from their ranks. Staff people expected Shawn to choose someone on the inside, perhaps Frank Modell. After the fact, it was learned that Shawn had indeed first offered the job to the magazine's senior fiction editor, Roger Angell.

Roger seemed a natural choice. He'd long been interested in the magazine's art, particularly the cartoons, and as an editor was instrumental in developing some of the magazine's most distinctive comic voices, including Woody Allen, Donald Barthelme, Marshall Brickman, Veronica Geng, Ian Frazier, and, later on, Garrison Keillor. Roger accepted, but he and Shawn could not agree on a satisfactory way to compensate Roger for the lost writing time and increased responsibility.

Mr. Shawn

The failure to reach agreement with Roger turned Shawn's attention to a small group of candidates, among them Charlie Barsotti, who had been cartoon editor at *The Saturday Evening Post* in the sixties; the cartoonist Ed Fisher; Geraghty's longtime assistant Barbara Nicholls; and Geraghty's choice, the cartoonist Don Reilly.

As one of the few cartoonists who had an office on the premises, I was assumed to be close to the situation and was constantly being asked to read the tea leaves. The truth is, I knew as little as anyone else. After weeks of this oppressive atmosphere of uncertainty and anxiety, Jim Geraghty invited me to join him in Shawn's office, where Shawn to my amazement offered the job to me.

Since people, especially people outside the magazine, often tell me that I have the best job in the world, it may be difficult to believe that I hesitated a week before accepting. But the art editor's job is, after all, 99 percent rejection, and the artists I would be dealing with were not only colleagues but friends. There was also the question of my own career as a cartoonist and an illustrator. Since I clearly could not edit my own submissions, Shawn agreed to assume that responsibility. This arrangement continued with Bob Gottlieb and Tina Brown.

Why Shawn offered me the art editorship is as much a mystery to me today as it was twenty-three years ago. After Shawn retired I asked him the question directly, but his answer was uncharacteristically vague. He did mention that I had been president of the Magazine Cartoonists Guild and that he wanted someone who knew the artists and was familiar with their problems. He also reminded me that, in fact, I had not been hired immediately, but merely had been invited to audition for the job. Over a transition period of three months I worked under Jim Geraghty's guidance, reviewing roughs, meeting the artists, and sitting in at the art meetings. Jim regularly reported on my performance to Shawn, and it was on the basis of these reports, rather than any intuition of Shawn's, that the decision was finally made.

It's also important to note that during this probation period I enjoyed the advice and support of Barbara Nicholls. Among Barbara's responsibilities had been the sale of originals, and in the fall of '73 she announced her intention to leave *The New Yorker* and open her own gallery. The Nicholls Gallery has been impressively successful, and Barbara has curated a number of shows for *The New Yorker* over the years, including the widely traveled retrospective of the sixties and, in 1994, the large Charles Addams exhibit at the New York Public Library. Replacing someone of Barbara's intelligence and experience was a formidable task, but I had an extraordinary piece of luck. A bright, attractive young woman, Anne Laux, later Anne Hall, who had occasionally filled in for Barbara when she was on vacation, worked in the offices of managing editor Robert Bingham. Anne had impressed me not only with her sensitivity to the art but with the skill and diplomacy with which she dealt with the artists. Bob very graciously allowed me to invite her to join me in the art department, where we have worked together for the last twenty-two years. Anne's intelligence, warmth, and commitment to the magazine and to the artists have made her an indispensable ally, and I don't believe that there is an artist who has not been nourished by her understanding and patience.

Disgruntled would-be contributors routinely accused *The New Yorker* of elitism, nepotism, and, more seriously, plagiarism. The standard cartoon categories are not infinite, and several artists often produce similar ideas. Most professional cartoonists make allowances for such redundancies, but I still run into people who believe that *The New Yorker* steals ideas, hides them in some subterranean vault for a year or two, and then passes them along surreptitiously to regular contributors. Common sense is a futile weapon against such deep-seated paranoia, and over the years I've accumulated a large file of letters, mostly unsigned, accusing us, or me, of such unsavory practices.

A unique example of this form of coincidence was provided by Henry Martin, who submitted the rough sketch reproduced at right the same day that the above drawing by Sid Harris appeared in the magazine.

To the extent that their work is topical, cartoonists are often merely vehicles of the zeitgeist. The first wave of anti-smoking sentiment produced these drawings by James Stevenson and Arnold Roth almost simultaneously in 1988. In 1993 similar news stories inspired Barry Blitt to produce an almost identical cover.

Jan. 10, 1994   THE   Price $2.50

NEW YORKER

At most magazines the responsibilities of the art directors include overseeing the magazine's physical look: designing pages, selecting photos, arranging type. When I followed Geraghty at *The New Yorker*, these responsibilities were handled by the make-up department, and the art editor's role was more like that of a fiction editor: helping the artist say what he was trying to say clearly, in his own voice. In a less elevated sense, the art editor's job was, and remains, to winnow down the massive pile of weekly submissions to an amount small enough for one man to carry to the weekly art meeting. This meeting is still held on Tuesday at two in the afternoon in the editor's office. When Shawn "vacationed" at his summer home in Bronxville, the material was shipped back and forth by messenger. I would bring to the art meeting (1) my selection of the most promising rough cartoon ideas, culled from both unsolicited and contract artists, (2) finished versions of ideas OK'd the previous week, (3) cover sketches by both new and established artists, and (4) examples of work by unpublished artists I thought we should consider encouraging. Once a month we would go through the spot drawings.

Under William Shawn, the editors never met as a group. Each department functioned as a spoke in a wheel, with Shawn as the hub. Even so, editors, including the art editor, did not operate in a vacuum. A survey of the weekly routine amply conveys the depth of the support available. Following the weekly art meeting, the finished drawings were examined by a representative of the fact-checking department and then passed along for a final OK from the legal department. The ideas OK'd at the art meeting were checked by the library against our published inventory, and returned to the art department. The following day, Wednesday, the OKs that passed muster were returned to the artists, either in person or by mail with appropriate comments and suggestions from me or from William Shawn. At

the same time, finished drawings purchased on Tuesday were being statted by the make-up department, in a variety of sizes, for the Wednesday morning sizing meeting. At that time this meeting was attended by Hobey Weekes, who slugged the drawings for timeliness, Carmine Peppe, head of the make-up department, and myself. Since payment was by the square inch, a great deal of ingenuity was displayed by the artists in producing drawings that only looked good when reproduced large.

Simultaneously the caption sheets, such as the example shown on the next page, were circulated to the copy editors and to Peter De Vries, whose responsibility went well beyond reshaping an awkward caption. The amusing memos concerning Hegel and Wittgenstein, though extreme, were not untypical.

Everything published in *The New Yorker* is carefully scrutinized by both the fact-checking department and the legal department. Routine suggestions—the placement of a button on a coat, the proper arrangement of a telephone cord—are usually accepted with good grace by the artists. On occasion, however, the zeal for correctness in the checking department runs head-on into what the artists feel is the free exercise of their muse. Although the artists sometimes grumble, I think it's important to note that over the years the checkers have saved them from much potential embarrassment with our sharp-eyed readers. When common ground cannot be established, the burden of responsibility is shifted from the checking department to the artist (or editor) by the initials *OTA*—"on the artist." By Thursday morning everything that had to be mailed out was mailed out, and the rest of the day was spent catching up with artists from out of town, either in person or by telephone. Thursdays also provided me with an opportunity to go through the portfolios of unsolicited material that had been dropped off the day before.

Helpful hints from the Checking Department:
Query sheet (right) for one panel of "Distressed Tableware" by Bruce McCall (below), and an opportunity to "correct" Roz Chast's Hungarian offered by the checker (below, bottom)

THE HARDING MINT PRESENTS
AUTHENTIC DISTRESSED TABLEWARE & CROCKERY
OF THE GREAT 19ᵗʰ CENTURY
U.S. VICE-PRESIDENTS

GRAVY BOAT:

The 1808 crockery gravy boat that Mrs. George Clinton found too hot not to drop at a state dinner for the Emperor of Brazil can now grace your home, office or den. Guaranteed damaged by painstaking secret "pre-cracking" process.

OH? The first emperor of Brazil took office in 1822 when Brazil achieved independence.
② Also, I don't know if the U.S. gave a state dinner for the Emperor of Brazil.

OH? I know that George Clinton married in 1770 but I don't know the date of Mrs. Clinton's death, i.e., I don't know if she was alive as late as 1808.

FOREIGN LANGUAGES 125

HUNGARIAN

A	a	o in dog	N	n	n
Á	á	a in father	NY	ny	ni (ny) in Virginia
B	b	b	O	o	o in horn
C	c	ts	Ó	ó	o in stone
CS	cs	ch in change	Ö	ö	u in purr
CZ¹	cz	ts in its	Ő	ő	eu in French peur ² ³
D	d	d	P	p	p
E	e	e in lend	R	r	r (trilled)
É	é	ai in wait	S	s	sh in shut
F	f	f	SZ	sz	s in silly
G	g	g in pig	T	t	t
GY	gy	d in duke, or j in joy	TY	ty	t (ty) in tune
H	h	h	U	u	oo in good
I	i	i in bits	Ú	ú	u in brute
Í	í	i in ravine	Ü	ü	u (y) of French nu, mue ¹ ²
J	j	y in yard			
K	k	k	Ű	ű	(²)
L	l	l	V	v	v
LY	ly	l (ly) in lute	Z	z	z
M	m	m	ZS	zs	French j

¹ Eliminated since 1910.
² No corresponding sound in English.
³ Really only lengthened form of preceding vowel.

The characters of the alphabet have sounds as shown in the table which never vary, and no character is ever silent.
Punctuation is practically the same as in English.

Capitalization

Forms of address in letters, etc., and titles are capitalized: *Felséges Uram* (Your Majesty); *Méltóságod* (Your Lordship).
Proper names and those referring to God are capitalized.
Adjectives formed from proper names are not capitalized: *budapesti* (of Budapest); *magyar* (Hungarian).

Syllabication

Simple words are divided at the end of a line so that where two vowels follow one another they are separated: *fi-am, mi-enk, ti-e-id.*
Where two consonants follow one another, they also are separated: *nap-pal, er-dő.*
Where a single consonant occurs between two vowels, it goes with the next syllable: *vá-ros, va-dász.* This rule also holds good where the consonant is a double one: *gy, cz, ly, ny, sz, ty, cs, zs* (*a-gyag, e-cset, e-czet, a-nya, a-tya, ró-zsa*).
Two combinations of consonants occurring together in one word are abbreviated: *ssz* instead of *sssz;* but when they are divided, the original spelling is restored: *hosz-szú.*
Compound words are divided according to their construction: *rend-őr, meg-áll.*

MORE N.A.T.O. ALTERNATIVES

The Music Appreciation Society

Every month, we'll send Hungary, for example, five great American CD's. Then they'll return the favor.

At right is the caption sheet for a cartoon by Bud Handelsman. Below is De Vries's amended caption, followed by a response from the artist.

"Yes, according to Kant, Hegel, or maybe even Schopenhauer, I might be held personally accountable, but before you go off the deep end read Wittgenstein."

Because Wittgenstein, as disciple of Bertrand Russell and emphasizer of the illusions created by the ambiguities of language etc., might make more of a case for the ethical relativity to which he's presumably enjoining his wife. More than Hegel I mean, with his absolute idealism.

DeV

March 25, 1981

Dear Lee,

First as regards Peter De Vries's suggestion: Kant believed profoundly in human autonomy, that is, that men are (or ought to be) free to act as they choose, and consequently are responsible for the choice they make. This isn't Schopenhauer's main concern, but as far as I know he doesn't challenge the idea. Hegel, although an optimist who believed that the human spirit is struggling upward towards the absolute ideal, is generally considered a determinist; we are in the grip of forces over which we have no control. If I've got it wrong, I apologize to all the philosophers whose names I've bandied about. If not, I prefer my version to Peter De Vries's. It isn't a matter of ethical relativity (Wittgenstein) but of determinism (Hegel—I could have said Marx, but didn't want any political implications).

Thanks for asking. I appreciate being consulted when a caption change is in the offing.

Bud

AF 3744

HANDELSMAN

Bot: 3/17/81

ANYTIME

"Yes, according to Kant, or even Schopenhauer, I might be held personally responsible, but before you go off the deep end read Hegel."

I'm not convinced that fantasies of worthlessness and rejection are more common among so-called creative people, but surely cartoonists have chosen a field where such fantasies are most easily triggered.

After I moved from the contributor's side of the desk to the editor's side, I discovered that the anxieties that I accepted as my own private demons were widely shared by my colleagues. This nightmare is as common among artists as dreams of forgetting your locker number is to the rest of America. The most chilling version I've come across was offered to me one day by the cartoonist William O'Brian. It goes like this: After years of my being published with some regularity by the magazine, the editor invites me into his office. He quietly closes the door and gestures me to a seat. Sweat trickles down my spine. My stomach knots itself into a ball. Finally, he speaks. For the last several years, he says, we have, with more generosity than common sense, allowed your drawings to appear in our pages. Although they often embarrassed us and outraged our readers, we hoped—unreasonably, in the event—that the quality of your work might improve. That expectation having been disappointed, it was our belief that some residual sense of decency would lead you to withdraw your work from consideration before we were forced to act as we must act now. Your continued appearance in our pages has gone beyond a question of charity to one of survival. The widespread revulsion with which readers respond to your work now threatens the life of our magazine, and by extension the livelihood of your colleagues. (I cannot say "peers.") Since you have not volunteered to do the decent thing, I must spell it out for you. In this envelope are the sketches which you left here last week, along with assorted rejects from the past. Take it and burn it. I suggest you do the only thing left to you to honor your profession—that is, remove yourself from it. Leave, and do whatever you can, as we will, to erase from the public record all evidence of your feeble, misguided attempt to become a comic artist.

Ironically, the demons that torment most artists seem to have spared Charles Addams. The adjectives that suit him are easygoing, lighthearted, urbane, and civilized. While many artists approach a drawing board as though it were the rack, Charlie always drew with easy confidence and obvious pleasure.

It will disappoint many of Charlie's fans to know that he enjoyed a spectacularly normal childhood in the blameless suburban community of Westfield, New Jersey. His father was trained as a naval architect and drew a bit, but the household does not seem to have been particularly artistic. Charlie began drawing by copying his favorite comic strips, "Skippy" and "Krazy Kat," and as a teenager he won first prize in a magazine contest with a sketch of a Boy Scout in rubber boots rescuing a worker from a fallen power line. The caption under this exemplary drawing was: "Be prepared." Charlie's prize was a gift certificate, with which he purchased not six sticks of dynamite and an alarm clock but a baseball glove. The link between art and commerce having been established, Charlie continued his art studies at Colgate, University of Pennsylvania, and finally the Grand Central School of Art, which was located just two blocks east of *The New Yorker*'s offices in Manhattan. His first submission to be published here—in 1932—was a spot, which he sold while he was still at art school. Over the next few years his sales grew so steadily that he was encouraged to abandon his job at *True Detective* magazine, where he removed blood from photographs, and concentrate on cartooning.

Charlie's first drawings for *The New Yorker* were simple line sketches. The elegant wash style, in which he rendered his most memorable pieces, had yet to be developed. There are echoes in these virtuoso performances of two of his early favorites, Doré and Rackham. But it's also possible that he was inspired by the masterful full-page drawings then appearing in the magazine by Richard Decker and Garrett Price.

Ross recognized early on a taste for the bizarre in Charlie's works, and he strongly encouraged it. It was also Ross who suggested Addams expand his first sketches of the Addams family into a long-running series. Oddly enough, the Addams family, which made him famous if not rich, represented but a small part of his output for the magazine, less than two dozen drawings all together. There undoubtedly would have been more, but one condition of the magazine's agreement to their being used as a basis for a TV series was the understanding that they would no longer appear in our pages. I should add that when Bob Gottlieb succeeded Shawn in '87, he tried to revive the family, but years of reruns had pretty much destroyed Charlie's taste for his own creation. Charlie's close friend Frank Modell once commented to me that Addams's work was in one sense primitive. This is certainly not to say it was unskilled. Many of Charlie's drawings required technical control beyond the range of self-taught or naive artists. On the other hand, like many primitives, Charlie emphasized the narrative rather than the virtuoso side of his art. Cartooning is, after all, storytelling, and Charlie was a master storyteller. He seemed to know instinctively how to arrange his players and a few simple props. The setting was always carefully drawn and lovingly rendered. Charlie had a lifelong interest in architecture. The characters are often doll-like, and even under the most strenuous circumstances—being chased by dragons, or throttled by an octopus—their gestures are contained, never melodramatic. The effect was often of a kind of puppet theatre, a Punch and Judy show, where the serious violence happens offstage.

Charlie once said to an interviewer, "I admire practical people. You have to have someone to set your ideas against." Practicality carried to extremes is a kind of madness. This is a theme that crops up again and again in Charlie's work. No matter how despicable their goal—the blowing up of the White House, or disposing of an irritating spouse—many of Charlie's protagonists are simply fuddled mortals trying to do a difficult job well.

I think the enduring fascination with Charlie's famous drawing of the skier derives from the same source. Her decision to plunge straight ahead, beyond all reason, is a triumph of determination over "common sense." It is preposterous but at the same time deeply satisfying. This drawing has been used in the Binet test for mental skills, and a learned paper in Germany declared that the humor could not be appreciated by anyone under the age of fifteen.

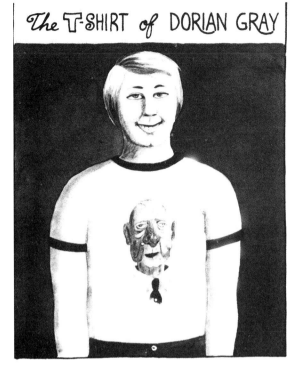

The T-SHIRT of DORIAN GRAY

"One more time."

Although over the course of his career Charlie occasionally drew ideas supplied by others, he was to the end a resourceful creator of his own material. In his later years he moved from the bizarre to the surreal—a development that was particularly appealing to then editor Robert Gottlieb.

In 1988, after a pleasant day spent in the country with friends, Charles Addams died in front of his New York apartment house, behind the wheel of one of his favorite antique cars.

In his tribute to Addams, Shawn wrote: "*The New Yorker* was not complete until Addams joined it." This is a puzzling statement for a man not given to hyperbole, but I think I know what Shawn meant. When Addams arrived *The New Yorker* was famous for cartoons that were clever, biting, topical, occasionally satirical, always sophisticated. What Charlie added were cartoons that were out-and-out funny. They were unexpected and sharp, but they were never unkind. In short, he brought to the magazine the best qualities of himself: a talented hand, a keen but forgiving eye, and boundless generosity of spirit.

"I knew about the wings, but the webbed feet are a surprise."

May 19, 1975 · THE NEW YORKER · Price 60 cents

Everyone seems to have a notion of what makes a *New Yorker* cover, but it would be difficult to find a common stylistic denominator in the works of, say, Arthur Getz, George Price, Ed Koren, Saul Steinberg, Gretchen Dow Simpson, Chuck Saxon, Peter Arno, and Constantin Alajalov. There is one thing, however, that these covers *do* share—each is clearly the work of a distinctive artistic personality. If the covers of the magazine carry any message, it is contained in this simple fact: they announce *The New Yorker* as a weekly forum for a wide range of distinctive talents; poets, writers, journalists, and artists come together to discuss, in their various voices, the issues of the day or yesterday or, occasionally, tomorrow.

To silence a persistent questioner, James Geraghty once defined a *New Yorker* cover as "Whatever I like." In fact, since *The New Yorker* did not at that time commission cover work, the covers could be more accurately described as representing what the artists liked. Until recently, the covers of *The New Yorker* never related to the editorial content of the magazine and often, with the exception of the changing seasons and the expected holidays, seemed to have little to do with the world outside the magazine. World War II, of course, was too large to be ignored, but in general the covers reflected the passing parade intermittently, if at all. The scale seemed either large and impersonal—Arthur Getz's cityscapes, Charles Martins's scenes of Central Park—or small-scale and private—the quiet humor of Mary Petty or the genre scenes of Edna Eicke. Covers that were essentially colored cartoons, such as this example by Whitney Darrow, Jr., continued to appear, but not as frequently as before the war.

The postwar *New Yorker* chronicled the rituals of suburban life: changing the screens, sending the kids off to camp, repainting the house, and inviting neighbors over for a barbecue.

The covers of the sixties reflect Geraghty's desire to "go toward the poster." A strong central image dominates many of these, an approach characteristic of some of the newer artists, particularly the European contributors André François, Jean-Michel Folon, and Ronald Searle. Joining the cartoonists who already did covers, such as Charles Addams and Helen Hokinson, was a new group of switch-hitters, including Donald Reilly, Anatole Kovarsky, Frank Modell, Chuck Saxon, and Jim Stevenson.

For most of the decade the list of cover artists was remarkably stable, from Addams and Alajalov through Birnbaum and Bemelmans to Steinberg, with occasional contributions from Robert Day, Richard Taylor, and Whitney Darrow, Jr. Over this period Arthur Getz, the most prolific of our cover artists, seems to have found his particular subject, the special light of Manhattan. He captured it in dozens of memorable covers, from the morning sun tinting the East River to the last flash of sunset across the Hudson. Most New Yorkers spend their time either indoors or underground, and it's easy to forget that we live on an island. Arthur's paintings are a chronicle of New York's moods to be set alongside Guardi's paintings of Venice.

June 8, 1987

THE NEW YORKER

Price $1.75

GRETCHEN DOW SIMPSON

The weekly portfolio drop-offs at *The New Yorker* were a convenience to those cartoonists I did not have time to see personally. They were also an opportunity for potential cover artists to allow us to view samples of their work. One of the first to catch my attention was work by a young woman named Gretchen Dow Simpson. I invited her to come in and discuss her work and discovered that she had been submitting to *The New Yorker* for several years. Her work combined a classical sense of design with a delicately modulated palette in a way I was confident would be appealing to Shawn. At the same time, I could see why her previous submissions had not been successful. Like most aspiring contributors, she'd studied the magazine carefully. As a result, her sketches were a kind of anthology of previously published work. The advice I gave her, which I have repeated many times but seldom with such immediate success, was to produce sketches for herself rather than for us. The next group of drawings she submitted included what would be her first cover to appear on *The New Yorker* magazine. Helping an artist grow is the most satisfying part of my job, and few artists have developed careers as gratifying to me as Gretchen's. From her early work—carefully outlined drawings colored in flat areas of acrylics—she has moved on to produce confidently rendered oil paintings. Her subject matter has broadened correspondingly, and today her work hangs comfortably on the walls of galleries and museums.

Over the next several years a large group of new cover people emerged from these weekly drop-offs, including Paul Degen, Robert Tallon, Heidi Goennel, Susan Davis, Iris Van Rynbach, and Barbara Westman. And even though Shawn discouraged jokes on the covers, the number of cartoonists drawing them grew as well—Robert Weber, Dean Vietor, George Booth, and Charlie Barsotti.

June 13, 1983 THE NEW YORKER Price $1.50

THE NEW YORKER

April 29, 1985 THE NEW YORKER Price $1.50

May 31, 1976 THE NEW YORKER Price 75 cents

PAUL DEGEN

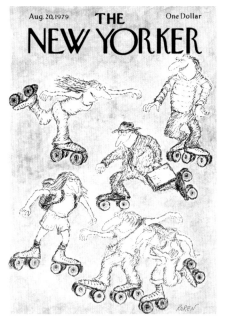

Although Shawn never articulated a general philosophy of covers to me, I knew he approved the answers I usually gave to questions on the subject. *The New Yorker*, being primarily a subscription magazine, as we were at that time, did not have to seize the buyer's attention on the newsstand. Since most people had the magazine around for a month or so, covers were, I hope, attractive enough to be part of one's living space for that period of time. The one point Shawn did make to me was that he felt the gag covers that characterized the magazine in the thirties, forties, and fifties were no longer appropriate, and the reflective tone of the covers from that period was clearly evident in *The New Yorker* cover book in the years 1970–85. Shawn also felt that our increasingly divided and dangerous world was well covered inside the magazine and that it was not necessary to reflect those concerns on the covers themselves.

For most of the magazine's history, the covers were never meant to be more than amusing and pleasing to look at. This does not seem to be enough for many of our readers. Long before teasing out the hidden "subtext" that lies below the innocent surface of life became a popular indoor sport, our readers began scrutinizing our covers with the same attention now reserved for such pop phenomena as romance novels and game shows.

One reader in particular has made a career out of reworking Jenni Oliver's covers and returning to us his version with her "mistakes" in perspective corrected on a transparent overlay.

The most unexpected and disturbing response to a cover was generated by an image by Charles Addams which appeared on the Thanksgiving issue, dated November 27, 1978. To us, this idea, a variation on a cartoon of his which had appeared many years earlier, seemed a clever twist, even a politically correct one, on the traditional view of turkey as victim. Several readers, however, to our shock and dismay, found the image evocative of Nazi concentration camps. Their reactions ranged from sorrow to outrage. This kind of thing can be contagious, and I found myself searching for hidden subtexts in the inventory. One day I was scheduling covers and noticed the one reproduced here by Charles Martin, scheduled for the issue of November 22, the date of the Kennedy assassination. While checking the proofs, a terrible suspicion crossed my mind. Could an imaginative reader, his fantasies triggered by the cover date, read references to the Kennedy assassination in what seemed to me an innocent drawing of a child's playground? Suddenly the whole thing came into focus. I noted four swings: three empty, one for Joe, Jr., one for Jack, one for Bobby; and on the fourth, a Teddy. I felt duty-bound to take my suspicions to Shawn. He listened po-

Even by the low-tech standards of *The New Yorker,* scheduling covers was a primitive operation. The scheduling boards, which I inherited from Jim Geraghty, were three 42-by-36-inch sheets of matboard. Each contained twenty sleeves, 6 by 8 inches, improvised out of cardboard and masking tape. These were designed and fabricated by Barbara Nicholls. When covers were purchased, in addition to the large black-and-white stats, which we kept in our file books, a pair of 5-by-6-inch stats were shot for use in the scheduling process, and these were filed in our cover bank, two large photo albums, one arranged by artist and one arranged by categories (that is, holidays, seasons, and so on). The originals of the art were stashed away in a fireproof vault on the eighteenth floor. By tradition, the bank contained about two years' worth of covers. Mr. Shawn allowed me to schedule the covers, although I always consulted with him on his holiday preferences.

The scheduling process began with setting the schedule boards up on a couch in my office. The previous months' covers were represented by black-and-white stats on the schedule boards so I could check for repetition in artist or subject matter. I would select from the stats about a dozen likely candidates, remove the originals from the vault, and carry them to my office. These I would shift back and forth until I felt the group had a pleasing sequence of styles, colors, and subjects. I would then attach to the back of each cover a schedule sheet giving the issue date, the price, the name of the artist, and a sample of the logo color. These were then sent along to the color separator. To determine the logo colors, I depended less on the samples supplied by the separator than on tear sheets from previous issues or, occasionally, on samples I would mix up myself.

Mr. Truax:

There follows some reflections by Mr. Geraghty on art rates. If everlasting thinking will get us out of the wilderness, we may get out.

"Whenever I think of increased rates for artists, I run up against the fear that while more money will induce some artists to work harder for us, it will make it possible for other artists to do less work. The obvious answer to this is a Bonus Plan. However, I think a bonus to work has to be really substantial, and artists whose volume of work is limited by shortage of ideas, difficulty with drawing, etc., would feel penalized. So also would these artists who are prepared to draw twenty pictures a year but can't find the time profitably to draw thirty-five. I propose for your consideration a plan under which we would offer all artists the choice of a straight rate or a bonus rate. The straight rate would be raise over the present rates. The bonus rate, if earned would amount to more per picture than the straight rate, but less per picture if the bonus is not earned.

"I also propose that the spread between 'AA' and 'A' artists' rates be increased.

"Now I return to my old argument that in classifying an artist we should take into consideration all phases of his talent rather than confine ourselves to appraisal of his drawing alone. Quality of ideas and flow of ideas is as important to the magazine (if not more important) as quality of drawing. An 'A' artist with lots of good ideas of his own is, for my money, more valuable than an 'AA' artist without any ideas.

"The 'art problem' in general baffles me. Perhaps there isn't any 'art problem'; at least any problem that can be solved with one policy

litely and then sensibly told me to turn my imagination to more productive areas. The cover ran. No letters were generated. I filed the occasion away in my bulging portfolio of synchronistic events.

Next to "What was Charles Addams really like?" the question I am most often asked is "What do *The New Yorker* artists make?" If the artists themselves were to be polled, I'm sure the answer would be, not nearly enough. The hard truth is that even a prolific contributor to the magazine makes barely enough to support the average family (that is, two adults and one-and-a-half children; two children would be out of the question). In our unending attempts to provide equitable rates, the pay scales have been recalculated many times. Ross initially established a per-square-inch rate, which meant that everything had to be sized before payment could be made. To encourage production, a quantity bonus for every ten drawings was added in the forties, when many cartoonists were making more money in advertising than at the magazine, and in the fifties a cost-of-living adjustment, or COLA.

Over the years the payment system has achieved Talmudic complexity. At the time I joined the magazine in 1958, all of the above, plus the contractual payment (a percentage of your gross average income over the previous three years), divided by the number of cartoons sold each year, would yield a per-drawing rate of approximately five hundred dollars. Cover artists at that time were paid a flat rate of fifteen hundred dollars, and spot drawings or spot-plus drawings (another complicated category) were paid for at a rate of thirty dollars. COLA was dropped during the inflation of the seventies, but the other figures have gradually moved upward over the years.

By the late eighties the complexity of the system made it impossible for most contributors to understand exactly what they were being paid. Bob Gottlieb attempted to cut this Gordian knot by eliminating the bonuses and creating an incremental pay plan. This has the advantage of clarity but, since it drops an artist's rates at the beginning of each year, is psychologically unsatisfactory.

We are now using so many kinds of art that most of these calculations seem beside the point. In the near future I expect we will establish flat rates in all categories.

For many *New Yorker* artists, there are two other potential sources of income. One is reprints and royalties. *The New Yorker* retains many rights in the drawings it publishes but has traditionally shared monies generated by these rights with the artist. These include royalties from *New Yorker* collections and fees collected for work reprinted elsewhere. The reprint department generates thousands of dollars in additional revenue each year for the artists and for other contributors. It is now in the capable hands of Jill Frisch and Grace Darby, but when I joined the magazine in 1958 it was run by the formidable Daise Terry. Her tour of duty as rights and permissions editor was marked by confusion, bad feeling, lost checks, and weeping secretaries. During my first years at the magazine I occasionally received calls from her office to solicit my agreement to a reprint request. (This was strictly pro forma, no artist ever said no.) I never received any checks from her office, however, and when I dropped by to question their whereabouts, I was invariably greeted by a blank stare. I would reintroduce myself. "Mr. Lorenz," she would say, "I thought you were an older man with a beard." I never identified the older man with a beard. I assume he is now living comfortably in the tropics on those reprint checks Miss Terry regularly forwarded to him.

The other potential source of income for *New Yorker* artists is the sale of originals, which remain the property of the artist. The market for original cartoon art has grown, if slowly, over the last twenty years. *The New Yorker* itself continues to act as an intermediary for the artists in sales of originals. Why original cartoon art is still a marginal category in the larger spectrum of collectible graphic art is a puzzle. I suspect that in spite of proselytizing by such institutions as the Museum of Cartoon Art and the Wilhelm Busch Museum in Germany, collectors will only come to value cartoon art after museum curators begin adding Arnos and Prices to their portfolios alongside Rowlandson and Gillray. Many important institutions in the United States, including the Smithsonian, Ohio State University, Syracuse University, and the New York Public Library, have and exhibit large collections of cartoon art. One can only hope that the imprimatur of such prestigious institutions will convince collectors that comic art is, yes, an important collectible art form.

Over the years *The New Yorker* had developed a re-

applied equally to all artists. My mind is always filled with a lot of separate 'art problems.' Hokinson needs ideas. Barlow needs ideas. Darrow needs time. Hoff needs patience. Steinberg needs excitement. Macdonald needs energy. Decker needs money. Dove needs health. Day needs a vacation. Steig needs a new editor. So does Arno. Garrett Price needs common sense."

H. W. Ross

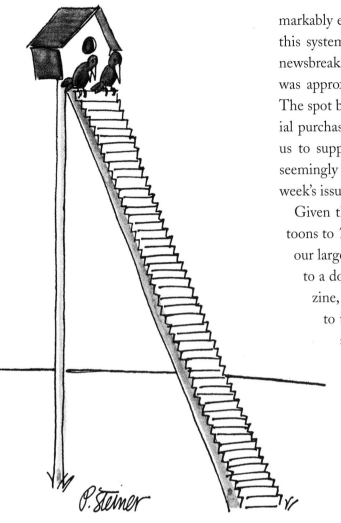

"It is a lot of steps, but it sure beats flying."

markably efficient system for producing a weekly magazine. The heart of this system is its huge, easily accessed inventory of fact, fiction, poetry, newsbreaks, spots, covers, and cartoons. At that time the cover inventory was approximately 130 pieces, and the cartoon bank approximately 550. The spot bank ran into the thousands. A short turnaround time—material purchased on Wednesday could run the following Monday—allowed us to supplement this large inventory with topical material. From this seemingly bottomless well, the editors would draw the material for each week's issue.

Given the diversity of the talents who over the years contributed cartoons to *The New Yorker*, it may be surprising to learn that everything in our large cartoon bank has, for the sake of easy reference, been reduced to a dozen or so categories. Over the years I've worked for the magazine, quarterly reports on the cartoon inventory were made available to the art editor and other interested editors. The categories were as follows: arts and galleries; bars and drinking; birds, fish, and animals; businessmen; cars and road signs; cavemen; children, babies, clergymen; cocktail parties; criminals, cops, jails, and judges; doctors and hospitals; heaven, hell, gods, devils, and so forth; olden times (royalty); old people; politicians and generals; musicians; restaurant and food; tourists, vacations; and finally TV and movies. As far as I know, we've never had anything in the bank that couldn't be easily fit into one of these categories. I'm sure the current bank contains a disproportionate number of TV and movie gags, whereas the cocktail party category is rather thinner than it used to be. Desert island and cavemen jokes, of course, go on forever.

"But can they save themselves?"

"Damn! I suppose this means another malpractice suit!"

"What about that day in 1922 when you said 'Shut up' to your mother?"

"How can I be sure you're a millionaire?"

"Damn it, I love you, don't you understand? How can you just sit there and read when you know how much I love you and want to go for a walk?"

"She's all work and no play."

"Wornal, take this plant out and kill it."

"Doesn't it strike anyone else as weird that none of the great painters
have ever been men?"

"Son, your mother is a remarkable woman." S GROSS

"If it please the Court, I have a get-out-of-jail-free card."

Even with the best will on both sides, the relationship between the magazine and its artists is a dicey one. Most contributors feel they don't sell enough. (It's true, they don't.) Or, if they happen to feel that their sales are satisfactory, that they don't appear often enough in the magazine. Or, if they appear often enough, that the drawings appear too small. Or, if the drawings are large enough, that they're too often in the back of the magazine and not often enough in "The Talk of the Town."

Shawn was often accused of buying work that he had no intention of running, just to keep contributors happy and eating. It is true that we stretched a point to help an artist over the inevitable dry spots, and as a contributor who likes to eat, I don't see anything wrong with that. The persistence of such rumors, however, was disturbing to stockholders. It's many years too late to reassure them, but for the record I can say that we never purchased any art we didn't feel we could publish. Every work purchased is an investment in an artist's talent and I cannot think of an artist in whom Shawn did not invest wisely.

"We located the hissing noise, Mr. Watkins. Your wife's mother is in the back seat."

Rarely, it seems, do the magazine and the artist agree on the relative merits of the work submitted. Each batch contains a few favorites. If these are passed over, they are likely to appear again and again in the hope that the editors will eventually come to their senses. Returning these favorite children to their parents without at the same time declaring them inferior requires the diplomatic skills of a Disraeli and occasionally the stone heart of a Genghis Khan. That the system has produced neither murder nor suicide can be explained by the tacit understanding that the passed-over work represents a failure not on the artist's part but on the editors'.

Next to outright rejection, the most delicate issue between the artist and the editor is the question of correcting a drawing. What I mean, of course, is improving a drawing. But since this implies some defect in the original artwork, "correcting" is the word most often used. When I took over from Jim Geraghty, my greatest anxiety was how to deal with the established artists over the question of correcting drawings. Alan Dunn, William Steig, Whitney Darrow, Jr., Mischa Richter, and Charles Addams were part of my graphic education. Saul Steinberg had seemed a god to me and was one of the saving presences of my dismal adolescence. Being a colleague of these artists had always seemed a kind of presumption. Editing their work seemed a new definition of chutzpah. Reading through Jim Geraghty's notes for his unpublished book on the magazine, I discovered that he found the problem equally daunting. Jim, as I knew from experience, had developed his own idiosyncratic and highly successful method of dealing with the situation. He would suggest some vague dissatisfaction in an uncharacteristically inarticulate way. As he fumbled to express himself, the artist was drawn into the search and more often than not identified the problem himself. This variation of the Socratic technique was a part of Geraghty's genius. Unfortunately, it was too familiar to the artists to be successfully used by me. Lacking Geraghty's ingenuity, I decided to make whatever suggestions I felt were necessary as directly as possible. To my surprise and relief, it worked. Every artist realizes how easy it is to spot the problem in someone else's drawing and how difficult it is to see the problems in one's own. I also had the advantage of being able to sketch out, as Geraghty could not, alternative solutions. In fact, my relationship with the established contributors was from the beginning remarkably smooth. I was, after all, only trying to get from them their best work. The editorial experience was a cooperative, not a competitive, venture. Their generosity of spirit quickly made me feel at ease, and working together to improve a drawing or cover helped me become a better editor of my own work.

Jim Geraghty was not always easy to please, but when he was pleased he expressed his feelings extravagantly. A particularly successful piece by one artist was often held up as an example to another. And as an idea man himself, he was always enthusiastic about a truly original idea. Jim's feelings were genuine, but his hyperbolic praise often made me uncomfortable. I assumed this was the case with the other artists. I was wrong. After I had been working as art editor for a few months, one of the artists asked if he could speak to me on a personal matter. "Personal matter" was usually a code phrase for money, and after I'd checked the balances in his account with the magazine's lawyer, Milton Greenstein, we set a time to meet. He entered my office and sat in silence for a few moments before he found the courage to speak. "Goddamn it," he said, "why don't you ever call me a genius?" I was stunned. It never occurred to me to call him or anyone else a genius. For Geraghty, it was a word that came easily to the lips and he used it often—more, I thought, as a way of prodding the less talented than praising the gifted. I tried to explain that my perceived lack of enthusiasm was merely a personality deficiency and not a measure of respect for the artist's work. In fact, the artist in question was one of the most gifted draftsmen and writers whom we regularly published. In my efforts to be constructive, I had not been sufficiently supportive. Although I'm still constitutionally incapable of gushing (Saul Steinberg once assessed my editing this way: "He is not a flatterer"), I'm grateful to this artist for reminding me that a little stroking is as important as plenty of the best advice.

When one considers all the competing demands brought into conflict in each week's issue, it is astonishing that anyone can be satisfied. And I think it's only fair to put in print the extent to which *The New Yorker* tries. The A-issue editor, the person responsible for the assembly of each week's issue, and the make-up department, which supervises the selection and placement of the drawings in the issue, each follows guidelines developed over the magazine's seventy years. The frequency of each artist's appearance is charted weekly, and is made to reflect his or her position in the inventory. The drawings are sized when purchased, the criterion being not how much space is available but in what proportion the drawing is most satisfactory. (It's not true that every drawing looks better printed as a full page.) Finally, the placement in the magazine, which some artists regard as a kind of rating system, is determined not by merit—they all have that—but by the relationship between the drawing and the surrounding text. Cartoons are never meant to illustrate a piece, and any echo, however remote, between the cartoon and a situation or a character in the text is scrupulously avoided.

For my first five years as art editor, Shawn and I had annual lunches at

Although Fiorello LaGuardia and Albert Einstein laughed and laughed and laughed at the joke, their socks did not fall down.

—"A Remarkable Friendship"
© 1971, He-Man Hose Manufacturing Company

Freud lay down on the lounge chair. The gentle buzzing of the mosquitoes soon lulled him to sleep, and he dreamed a dream that would change the face of psychology forever.

—"Interpretation of Freud"
© 1958, Lawn Chairs Unlimited of Pasadena

Villa readjusted his sunglasses against the blazing Mexican noon and stared out across the vast expanse. "So this is it," he murmured. "The whole enchilada."

—"Pancho Villa: The Action Years"
© 1963, Sun-Ban Company

the Algonquin. Over his toasted pound cake, Shawn was unfailingly generous in his assessment of my performance. We discussed new artists, the problems and achievements of the previous year, and the prospects for the year upcoming. Remarkable as it may seem, we never discussed the exact nature of my responsibilities as art editor. My "trial" period was inevitably extended. In fact, I was never officially hired, and after twenty-two years, I have now moved from the world's longest probation period into semi-retirement.

What was clear early on, and what made it possible for me to do my job successfully, was a deep, instinctive rapport with Shawn. He believed that the magazine should be shaped not by the editors but by the talents of its contributors. He felt the magazine was kept vital and growing by the influx of fresh talent, and was always eager to see interesting new work. In the seventies there was clearly a new breed of cartoonist developing, and *The New Yorker* and Shawn were quick to embrace them. The first new face I brought to the magazine was Jack Ziegler in 1974. Jack's drawings, which often used the conventions of the traditional comic strip as part of the joke, were unlike anything else I saw in my weekly romp through the slush pile. Headings were often substituted for the traditional gag line. Shawn and I agreed on the importance of his work and we began purchasing it. Weeks passed and Jack politely pointed out that he was still waiting to see himself in print. The bottleneck turned out to be Carmine Peppe. Jack's work did not satisfy Mr. Peppe's conception of the traditional *New Yorker* cartoon.

When my attempts to convince Carmine that we did indeed wish to publish these drawings failed, I turned to Mr. Shawn, who intervened. Peppe shook his head sadly but capitulated. In his eyes, we were moving down a slippery slope, and subsequent events only confirmed his suspicions. Other new faces followed, Bernie Schoenbaum, who was recommended to me by R. O. Blechman; then Dean Vietor, a refugee from Hallmark Cards; and eventually Roz Chast.

Roz's work arrived among the weekly drop-offs, and it was immediately clear to me that she was something special. Shawn shared my enthusiasm, although he asked me, "How does she know these are cartoons?" Indeed, Roz's drawings looked more like illustrated pages torn from an eccentric's diary than traditional gag cartoons. In fact, her work, despite its Beckett-like spareness, often reflects the homely concerns of her quiet suburban life: learning to drive a car, the competing demands of art and motherhood. We issued her a contract almost immediately. This time, Carmine Peppe was not alone in disapproving. Readers, staff members, and, I'm sorry to say, some cartoonists shared with me their negative reactions, which ranged from bafflement to outrage. In retrospect, it was clear that Roz's work was not a fluke but merely the most original example of a new sensibility which began to emerge in the seventies. It's worth noting that her work and Jack's seemed to widen the range of what the cartoonists considered possible. This included Roz's first inspiration, Charles Addams.

THE GIRL WITH THE
SENSIBLE SHOES

MANKOFF

"Captain, this Brie is totally out of control!"

Finding new work for old hands is also part of the editor's job. George Booth's rapidly expanding repertory company seemed to require a broader field. My suggestion that he try some extended pieces led to such spreads as "Keeping Warm," "Keeping Going," and eventually his unique and delightful "Ip Gissa Gul." This Stone Age comic strip is written in an ingenious yet decipherable argot, reminiscent of Burgess's *A Clockwork Orange*. Both Shawn and I found this offbeat and amusing, but neither of us had anticipated the response it would evoke from our readers. "Ip" has been turned into a drama, used as a teaching tool, set to music and performed by a church choir. The special appeal of these pages remains mysterious. George Booth, a man who wisely avoids heavy self-analysis, merely shrugs his large shoulders. He did, however, add "Ip" and his companions to his ever-growing stock company of comic creations.

To René-Alexis de Tocqueville
27, place de la République

Dear René-Alexis,

I thought a great deal on the airplane about the proposal you made to me the night before I left for NEW YORK.

What an honor for me to contribute, however modestly, to the book you've decided to write about the United States, so many years after your illustrious ancestor!

I'm going to send you, just as it happens, an account of my stay in NEW YORK, and maybe you'll be able to pick up here and there a few bits of information for your work.

Your devoted friend,

Jean-Paul Martineau

Although the core of *New Yorker* contributors had been developed here at the magazine, there have been occasions when artists well established elsewhere have been featured: André François, Ronald Searle, of course, R. O. Blechman, and, most recently, Ed Sorel and Art Spiegelman. Since at that time in the seventies, *The New Yorker* was not commissioning work, approaching an established artist and asking him or her to work on spec was a delicate business. I knew Shawn shared my enthusiasm for the French artist Jean-Jacques Sempé, but how to approach him was a puzzle. The solution, it turns out, was right next door or, at least, down the hall. Sempé had two close friends at *The New Yorker*. The reporter Jane Kramer and the artist Ed Koren, who had studied printmaking at the Atelier 17 in Paris several years earlier and spoke excellent French. Through them an introduction was arranged. Jean-Jacques, it seems, had long desired to appear in *The New Yorker* but was reluctant to trust his works to the vagaries of the French postal system. His first submissions, in fact, were carried to New York by me

Like my friends, the weather here is constantly changing. On the news this morning, for example, it was announced that there would be a brief but heavy downpour during rush hour. Foolishly, I'd not paid attention, but at the second drop on the sidewalk someone with more foresight than I appeared and offered me, for a very modest sum, an umbrella.

after our initial meetings in Paris. J.J. was passionate about New York City and determined to make his drawings as completely American as possible. His ambition, he told me, was to know the city well enough to invoke it in the few simple lines with which he could now suggest his home city, Paris. J.J. is an excellent writer as well as an artist and I suggested he combine both talents in a series of travel sequences about a Parisian alter ego here in Manhattan. The result was a group of beautiful spreads we called "Par Avion." (This perfect title was suggested by Roger Angell.) Since J.J.'s English is just slightly worse than my French, we agreed that he would write his pieces in French. These I had translated into English by a member of the French consulate. I then reworked this literal draft into what I hoped was a more colloquial New York idiom. The final version was of course sent to Jean-Jacques for his approval.

In no time at all, the downpour stopped, driven away by a rather violent wind, which tore my umbrella and blew it inside out. I'd wanted to bring it along to you in Paris, and I was a bit annoyed.

I turned to take the umbrella back, but the seller, like the weather, had altogether changed. He was now offering watches, again for a modest sum. I bought one, and thought of what my friend Bellerin-Bouvard is always saying: In New York, the more things change, the more nothing is the same.

À bientôt,
Jean-Paul

Jim Stevenson constantly produced more work than we could publish. He did spots, covers, "Talk" pieces, cartoons, spreads, profiles, fact pieces, casuals, and reportage. In fact, with the assistance of a checker or two, Jim could have easily turned out the magazine all by himself. The spreads he produced in the sixties and seventies have never been matched for variety and inventiveness, and the one reproduced here provoked a response from our readers almost as intense as "Ip."

Given the demographics of *New Yorker* readers, well-heeled and college-

THE BRUCKNER OCTAGON

A NEW book, "The Bruckner Octagon," by E. Powers Jackson, has brought to light an astonishing and frightening phenomenon: a series of baffling disappearances within a general area of New York known as the Bruckner Octagon. This section, vaguely eight-sided, includes Bruckner Boulevard, the Cross Bronx Expressway, the Bronx-Whitestone Bridge, the Mosholu Parkway, and the Hutchinson River Parkway, as well as other major arteries, and extends to the east as far as Pelham Manor. For many years, travellers in this area have felt a strange uneasiness, without knowing quite why. Rumors of the odd disappearances have generally been discounted or ignored by the media and others. When, for example, it was noted, at the opening of the giant Co-op City apartment complex, in 1968, that there were only forty apartment buildings instead of the scheduled forty-one, the missing building was "written off" by authorities as a simple, though embarrassing, blueprint error. Today, in the light of other strange vanishings, the Co-op City case cries out for reëxamination.*

Although some experts draw parallels between the so-called Bermuda Triangle, in the Atlantic Ocean, and the Bruckner Octagon, there are important differences, suggesting that entirely separate forces are at work, or at least forces "wearing a different hat." Author E. Powers Jackson points out in his book that the Bruckner mysteries usually share one common thread: the disappearances involve solid, basically immovable objects, primarily real estate.

Jackson offers in his book some striking photographic evidence; although the pictures are in some cases fuzzy or vague, they are nonetheless disturbing.

---

*The earlier disappearance, in the same area, of a large amusement park called Freedomland has also been ignored. This, too, should be checked.

EXAMPLE 2. Author Jackson states that six feet of the Bronx River Parkway near Gun Hill Road "vanished" during the night of March 11, 1971. Highway authorities deny this but admit "we have no way of knowing," adding, "In any case, there's always some shrinkage during cold weather."

EXAMPLE 1. Abandoned car. Regular travellers on the Hutchinson River Parkway and other arteries customarily pay little heed to abandoned cars on the roadside, noting only that each day these vehicles have fewer and fewer parts, until one day they are actually "gone." This phenomenon is routinely attributed to vandalism, but new theory suggests that something much more puzzling—indeed, alarming—is involved.

EXAMPLE 3. This roadside eatery stood at the southeast corner of Van Cortlandt Park until 7:29 A.M. of June 2, 1973, according to Jackson. Onetime residents of the area hold conflicting views. Some state that Howard Johnson's restaurants "all look alike," while other residents simply "don't want to get involved."

educated, the number who have mistaken parody for fact is surprisingly high. The all-time record for such confusion surely belongs to Jim Stevenson's spread on the Bruckner Octagon which ran April 7, 1975. A seemingly obvious parody of the Bermuda Triangle, it generated dozens of letters from puzzled and sometimes frightened readers, flying-saucer buffs, the psychic-phenomenon crowd, and newspaper and television reporters around the country.

Obviously the ghost of Orson Welles still stalks the land.

WHERE ARE THEY TODAY?

Above: Claremont Park power station.

Below: Pelham motel.

THE evidence goes on. Extraterrestrial mischief? Satanic intervention? Psychokinetic maneuverings? Author Jackson suggests several hypotheses, including "soft spots" in the Bronx (some experts think that a certain patch of concrete in a field near the Hutchinson River Parkway is the actual roof of the missing Co-op City building), molecular stretch (a gradual separation of particles until they no longer form a recognizable mass; in such an instance, a Howard Johnson's would "occupy" an area of several thousand miles, and hence be unidentifiable at any particular point), and even structural-fatigue interchange (SFI), a process believed to occur when a building, for example, can no longer "hack it" as a car wash and opts for a "simpler" existence as, say, a beach plum.

Perhaps the most frightening—indeed, devastating—piece of evidence in support of the Octagon theory was supplied by author Jackson himself. On the morning of January 3, 1974, Jackson was about to enter his garage on Tremont Avenue, prior to getting into his Volkswagen and driving to Orchard Beach to "check out a new lead" in preparation for an appearance later in the day on the "Merv Griffin Show." Jackson was in high spirits, and his wife, Sarah Ann, decided to take a couple of "snaps." "It's all coming together now," said Jackson jubilantly as his wife focussed the camera. They were his last words.

—JAMES STEVENSON

Above: E. Powers Jackson, 8:05 A.M.

Below: 1/50 second later.

Rumors that the magazine would be sold surfaced frequently during the eighties and were as regularly refuted by Milton Greenstein or, if the rumor persisted, William Shawn. Neither the staff nor the contributors took any of this very seriously, with the exception of the knowing few who were carefully following the reports of the magazine's annual meetings. The phenomenal profits of the sixties had slowed by the seventies, and by the eighties, though the stock was still selling at a premium, some board members were becoming uneasy about the diminishing number of ad pages. The remarkable story of poor management, poor timing, and just plain bad luck that eventually led to the sale of the magazine to S. I. Newhouse's Advance Publications has been widely chronicled in the press and in the book *The Last Days of The New Yorker*. For our story the important part is that most of the changes which followed had less to do with the change of ownership than with *The New Yorker*'s shifting fortunes within the magazine field. Although *The New Yorker* has often been treated and sometimes has even presented itself as a kind of public institution, it is, after all, a commercial business enterprise, and in the eighties business was not good.

To survive under the Fleischmanns or under the Newhouses or under anyone else, *The New Yorker* would have to adapt to a marketplace that had changed radically over a very short period of time. When I entered the cartoon field in the late fifties, the market included such mass-circulation magazines as *Collier's*, *Look*, *The Saturday Evening Post*, *Saturday Review*, as well as the Sunday supplements *This Week* and *Parade*. By the end of the sixties only *Parade* was left. Television had become the medium of choice for mass-circulation advertising and the national general-interest weeklies disappeared. For a while *The New Yorker* profited from this situation. The competition for the remaining advertising dollars became increasingly fierce. *The New Yorker* is an expensive magazine to produce, and the bills, like most magazines', are paid by the advertisers, not the subscribers. (When *The Saturday Evening Post* folded, its circulation was at an all-time high.) Change was being called for, but could it be effected without changing the unique character of the magazine? Newhouse bought the magazine on the assumption that it could. Almost ten years and three editors later, the answer is still not clear.

The question of the "succession," as Shawn's retirement was called around the magazine, had been the subject of conversation as early as the sixties. Among the names often mentioned then were Robert Bingham, Gardner Botsford, and Roger Angell. With the issue still unresolved in the eighties, and S. I. Newhouse growing anxious, Shawn himself put forward the name of Jonathan Schell.

Jonathan was widely respected as a writer. His "Notes and Comment" pieces on Vietnam and Watergate were notable for their intellectual passion, and his reflections on the future of the planet, published as "The Fate of the Earth," had earned him a large and faithful audience. However, many of the staff felt he lacked the necessary editorial experience, and there were similar feelings about Shawn's subsequent candidate, Bill McKibben. Shawn's next nominee, fiction editor Chip McGrath, was widely seconded.

Most people thought Chip was an excellent choice. He was young enough to satisfy the business side's call for youth, and sufficiently well-marinated in the lore and rituals of the magazine to satisfy both the older editors and the subscribers. As plans for the transfer of editorship moved forward, S. I. Newhouse made an announcement, on January 12, 1987, that shocked everyone. We were told that he had decided to replace William Shawn with the president and editor in chief of Alfred A. Knopf, Robert Gottlieb.

The choice of Gottlieb was widely discussed in the press, but the most heated conversations were within the magazine. The staff was stunned by Shawn's dismissal and astonished at Newhouse's choice of successor. Bob's achievements in publishing at both Simon & Schuster and Knopf were impressive, and in Mr. Newhouse's comments to both the press and the staff he emphasized Bob's lifelong love of the magazine and his warm relationship with many members of the staff.

On the other hand, Bob had had no previous experience in magazine publishing. A curious conversation I had with Shawn, shortly after his departure from the magazine, suggests there may have been another dimension to Newhouse's decision. When Newhouse informed Shawn that he was replacing him with Bob Gottlieb, Shawn expressed astonishment that an editor with no magazine experience would be chosen. Newhouse, according to Shawn, acknowledged the point, but also suggested that Shawn and Gottlieb shared a quality equally as important. When Shawn asked what that quality was, Newhouse replied, "Charisma." Shawn was taken aback. He claimed that he himself had never had charisma. Newhouse replied that, yes, in fact, he did have charisma, and since Gottlieb also had charisma, he was convinced that Bob was the logical choice. This is a very puzzling conversation. After thinking it over, I've decided that what Newhouse meant by "charisma" was a certain star quality, which, in the eyes of the media, Gottlieb and Shawn *did* share.

Even when he was being criticized, Shawn was, after all, an extraordinary presence in the magazine field, as Bob Gottlieb was an extraordinary presence in the book-publishing field. That Newhouse felt this characteristic was central to one's success as editor of *The New Yorker* is an interesting point. It does suggest that part of the owner's intention was to create new excitement in the media about the magazine, and that he felt that by choosing a person who had already generated in his own way a great deal of media excitement, he could bring this about.

Speculation about Bob's intentions echoed down the hallways and it was not encouraging. In this atmosphere of resentment and anxiety, a petition was circulated demanding that Bob renounce the offer from Newhouse, which he had already accepted. As a representative of the artists, I was urged to sign, and to gather as many additional signatures from the artists themselves as possible. Though I shared deeply the feelings of the rest of the staff, I hesitated. It didn't seem fair to drag the artists into this dispute. Beyond that, I felt that Bob Gottlieb was the wrong target for the staff's anger. It was, after all, S. I. Newhouse who had dismissed Shawn, and who seemed to have ignored an agreement which guaranteed that the choice of a successor would be discussed with the staff.

With misgivings, I declined to sign the petition, and in a note to Shawn attempted to explain the reasons for my decision. I think my decision was the right one, but I'm sure that Shawn, though he responded with characteristic generosity to my note, was hurt by this perceived failure to support him. In any event, my own feelings were still deeply conflicted when I had my first meeting with Bob, in his office at Knopf. He only increased my discomfort when he greeted me by saying, "Ah, the voice of sanity." I felt it necessary to spend our first ten minutes together explaining that my reluctance to protest publicly his selection as editor was not the same as an enthusiastic endorsement. Bob, however, was much more interested in discussing art than personalities.

Despite the uproar in the press and at the magazine, Bob seemed upbeat and was eager to talk about the future. He attempted to ease any anxieties I had by stressing his informed interest in the art at Knopf, and the happy relationships that he enjoyed with his art directors.

A glance around Bob's office suggested the range of his interests and achievements. The walls were lined with hundreds of books he had shepherded through the press, many by *New Yorker* writers. Relief was provided by a few notable busts of Elvis and other odd bits he had harvested on his regular trips to flea markets.

Our meeting lasted about an hour, at the end of which most of my questions about Bob's view of the magazine's art were still unanswered. We did, however, cover some essential points, and these I tried to present in the most positive way in a subsequent note on the meeting I mailed to the artists.

I did not meet Bob again until he and his executive editor, Martha Kaplan, whom he planned to bring to the magazine with him, joined me and Shawn at one of our last art meetings. Finally, I thought, I would gain some insight into Bob's plans for the magazine's art. Again I was disappointed.

Shawn presided, and Bob and Martha were polite and deferential. I thought they had been invited as participants, but, as Bob later told me, they believed they were invited only as observers. (Five years later, at our first meeting with Tina Brown, Bob went to special lengths to clarify the ground rules.) As a result of this confusion, the meeting was punctuated by awkward silences, which grew longer and more painful as the afternoon progressed. I began, as usual, with the covers. I had a finish by Gretchen Dow Simpson which we purchased and a few sketches of hers, one of which we OK'd. Shawn and I ordinarily viewed spots once a month, but since I wanted Bob to have a sense of the entire range of the art meeting, I brought a small sample to this meeting. Shawn and I went through these quickly, and he OK'd them all. Bob and Martha remained silent. At this point, as we prepared to go through the finishes from the previous meeting, even Shawn was beginning to look uncomfortable. Mercifully, it was an uncharacteristically small group. A drawing by George Price finally elicited a comment from Bob; he had edited one of his collections at Simon & Schuster. The silence that followed this remark only served to raise the discomfort index. We examined the rest of the finishes, each of which Shawn carefully initialed on the back, and then turned to my weekly selection of roughs. At this point, I think all parties would have been glad to separate. There being no graceful way to do so, however, we plunged into the roughs.

This was the point in our weekly get-togethers that Shawn enjoyed the most. Topics touched on in the cartoons, and sometimes the cartoonists themselves, were occasions for his reflections on everything from the rise of the food culture—he felt it was the one area in which the upwardly mobile young could outspend their parents—to the recent films of Robert Altman, but this afternoon Shawn limited himself to a simple yes or no on each sketch. The rest of the meeting swam by in a fog of anxiety and embarrassment. I said good-bye to Shawn, Bob, and Martha and scurried back to my office. Anne Hall, my assistant, was waiting outside her office to ask me how it went. "Like a bad blind date," I replied.

My desire for insight into Bob's taste was not fulfilled until a few weeks

Self-portrait by Lothar Baumgarten

Self-portrait by Jane Dickson

later when we met without Shawn to go through the cover and cartoon banks. It was quickly apparent that we would work amicably together even though Bob's style was radically different from Shawn's.

Bob's arrival was preceded by rumors of dire editorial changes—photography running on the covers, dropping cartoons, going biweekly—in fact, his innovations were carefully thought out and cautiously executed. Bob enlisted as an art adviser Rochelle Udell, associate editorial director at Condé Nast. Rochelle, like her superior, the legendary Alexander Liberman, worked as a kind of troubleshooter for the whole range of Condé Nast publications. (*The New Yorker* is legally not a part of the Condé Nast group, but both are under the corporate umbrella of S. I. Newhouse's Advance Publications.) Rochelle spent several weeks on the premises talking to editors, making design suggestions to the make-up department, and soliciting suggestions from other members of the staff, including myself.

Rochelle seemed to have a wonderful sense of the *New Yorker*'s traditions as well as its current problems, and her design suggestions, most of them too subtle to be noticed by the average reader, gave the front of the book a cleaner, airier look. In terms of the magazine's art, one of Bob's most important innovations was his decision to change the "Goings On" department from a service section to an editorial feature in 1989. (This index to local entertainment had been part of the magazine from the beginning. Shawn often expressed irritation with it, but never discovered a graceful way to drop it.) Bob added short reviews, sidebar features such as "Edge of Night Life," and illustrations, particularly caricatures.

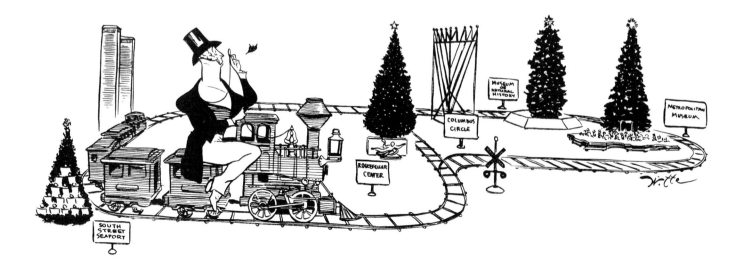

YOUR SENSE OF HUMOR ENABLES YOU TO GLIDE THROUGH LIFE'S DIFFICULT PERIODS.

Self-portrait by Alexis Smith

Ralph Giguerre

To assist with the expanded art needs of this section, he hired, at the recommendation of Rochelle Udell, a young woman from Condé Nast named Christine Curry, who had a fine arts background that Rochelle felt would be useful in dealing with Bob's new ambitions for G.O.A.T., as he dubbed the "Goings On About Town" department. Bob's partner in reinventing this section was Ingrid Sischy, who had been editor of *Artforum* and who would later become editor of *Interview*. After the traditional Tuesday art meeting, where Bob and I discussed covers and the cartoons, Bob would meet with Rochelle, Ingrid, and Chris to examine the finishes for each week and discuss assignments for the following week. The art included portraits, caricatures, and spot drawings, as well as some innovations. Ingrid encouraged friends from the art community to contribute self-portraits, and Bob hired the cartoonist Michael Witte to create weekly adventures for Eustace Tilley. (This move outraged many old-time *New Yorker* readers, but in fact, Shawn himself had long considered Tilley more of an albatross than an icon. As each anniversary approached, I'd delay scheduling the cover until I'd received the go-ahead from Shawn. His attempts to find a graceful way to retire Eustace Tilley often pushed up against the scheduling deadline, but inevitably the last-minute reprieve would arrive and the cover would run once again.)

Although the covers and the cartoons at *The New Yorker* were still being submitted on spec, the illustrations for "Goings On" were commissioned, a policy more reminiscent of Ross's magazine of the twenties than Shawn's magazine of the seventies.

ON THE THIRD DAY OUT OUR MORALE
WAS DEALT A CRUSHING BLOW

Bob quickly made it clear that he wanted to move away from what he felt were mined-out cartoon categories: kings and queens, knights and dragons, etc. This, combined with his quirky, idiosyncratic sense of humor, temporarily threw the artists off stride, and during the first few months the inventory shrank ominously.

As I struggled to help Bob and the cartoonists find common ground—I often felt like a marriage counselor who was seeing each spouse separately—we were extremely fortunate in recruiting some new cartoonists to the staff. Two new artists joined us from the West Coast. Stephanie Skalisky, whose work I had noticed while touring with *The New Yorker* Sixtieth Anniversary Show, and Bruce Eric Kaplan (B.E.K.). Bruce's carefully outlined sketches, invariably contained in a rectangular box, had an offbeat, retro look that Bob found compelling. There was also Victoria Roberts. Victoria is a performance artist as well as a cartoonist, and in her work Bob recognized a combination of elegantly stylized drawing and extravagant fancy that echoed his own taste for Glen Baxter and Edward Gorey. Contributors Richard Cline and Michael Maslin began publishing regularly about this time. It's also worth noting that Edward Sorel's work first appeared in our pages under Bob.

Bob's favorite new contributor, however, was a young man named Danny Shanahan. Danny is further proof, if any is needed, that only talent is required to get into *The New Yorker*. Danny, a remarkably normal young

KONG FOR A DAY

LASSIE! GET HELP!!

man, lives with his wife and children in Albuquerque, New Mexico, and for the first eight months of his career here, we worked together solely through the mail. His off-the-wall wit and shameless punning delighted Bob and also found a ready audience among our readers.

After six months, during which we bought fewer covers and cartoons than we were publishing, our weekly purchases began to rise. The artists began to produce work to Bob's taste, and Bob's taste seemed to broaden to encompass work he had previously passed by.

Bob and I generally got along well, even as we disagreed, as we did over one artist, Glen Baxter.

Baxter's drawings were catnip to Bob, and he had published several collections of them at Knopf. Glen's work is a highly personalized blend of stylized sketches seemingly derived from penny dreadfuls, and captions written in an arch and elaborate style. The humor is elusive; either you get it or you don't, and I didn't. I told Bob it seemed to be an acquired taste, which I probably would not live long enough to acquire. I also suggested that if it was important for him to run Baxter in the magazine, that he edit the drawings himself, since I felt I could not bring anything to the material. He agreed, and we did. I should add that though Glen's work still baffles me, I subsequently met him on a trip to London and discovered him to be personally as direct and charming as his work is mannered and enigmatic.

"Actually, I was assigned to Heaven, but it would have meant spending eternity with my first wife."

"Please let me through gentlemen I'm a dental hygienist."

SURPRISE PARTY

"Personally, I prefer a piano bar."

"It's pronounced '*hee*-la' monster. The 'g' sounds like an 'h.'"

"One side looks shorter than the other, don't you think?"

"I'd like to give you a break, but we did have you doing a hundred and eighty-six thousand miles a second on the radar."

"Someday man will find a peaceful use for my machines."

In conversations with Bob about design changes, I mentioned the extensive redesign project that Shawn and I had carried out in the late seventies. The magazine at that time was moving from hot type to film—undoubtedly, the last major magazine to do so. At the same time, a shift in press requirements demanded an adjustment in the magazine's proportions. It seemed the moment to reconsider other aspects of *The New Yorker*'s long-established look. And with Shawn's encouragement I hired a well-known designer named Robert Hallock. His assignment was to consider all aspects of the magazine's graphics, including typography and layout, and present us with a range of options. From a complete makeover to a bit of fine-tuning. Not surprisingly, after almost a year of discussions, we settled on the latter. The Irvin alphabet that we had used for headings was redrawn (the originals were lost, and over the years the metal plates had cracked and worn). The title page was redesigned and the margins were adjusted to compensate for the narrower page size. *The New Yorker* logo, which was appearing in six different faces, was made to conform throughout the magazine. The resulting changes, though significant when examined closely, were never commented on by our readers, our contributors, or the press.

My questions about Bob's attitude toward the magazine's art were being rapidly answered. Where Shawn wanted understated covers, Bob wanted covers that clanged like fire alarms. Shawn liked covers that were delicate and quietly amusing, but he avoided jokes. Bob loved jokes on the covers, as well as visual puns. Bob also had, of course, a notable taste for whimsy, something completely beyond Shawn's understanding. When it came to spots, Shawn preferred simple line drawings, whereas Bob was willing to experiment. Bob, with Ingrid's assistance, created a new kind of spot—a combination of line work and photography. Often these were overlooked gems of New York architecture, and they became a regular feature of "Talk."

An equally significant change was Bob's involvement with the production side of the magazine. Under Shawn, I had scheduled and color-corrected the covers, worked directly with the make-up department on layouts, and sized the art. Bob participated actively in all these areas and in addition supervised the selection and proofing of illustrations for the "Goings On" department. Bob's interest in design extended to the look of each page, and he worked closely with the make-up department, selecting, sizing, and placing the art. Bob had overseen the design and production of book covers at Knopf and was used to demanding and receiving perfection. Bob's requests for revisions, his determination to get it absolutely right, often pushed us right up against production deadlines.

Much of our early art meetings was given over to the search for new artists, as indicated above, but Bob also encouraged fresh approaches from established contributors. One who seemed to gain renewed vigor with Bob was William Steig.

"I was beginning to look like an artist."

Captain Blood

William Steig was born in Manhattan and grew up in the Bronx in a household that took both politics and art seriously. His parents, both ardent socialists, were from Poland. His father was a housepainter and gave his Sundays over to copying picture postcards in oils. Bill had three brothers, all of whom were gifted. The oldest, Irwin, was a newspaper writer. His brother Henry played the saxophone in vaudeville and later wrote up some of these experiences for *The New Yorker*. And his younger brother, Arthur, seems to have been the most politically advanced. According to Bill, he was reading *The Nation* while he was still in the cradle.

Bill studied art in high school and at City College, and later at the National Academy of Design. The need to add something to the family budget during the dark days of the Depression and the ready market for cartoon drawings led him into this field in 1930. In addition to *The New Yorker*, he published in *Collier's* and *The Saturday Evening Post*. When *The New Yorker* began publishing his work, his affectionate sketches of working-class families, culminating in the celebrated "Small Fry" drawings, quickly became features of the magazine.

"To a great human being!"

Spare Tire

HOOLIGAN

Hooligan

Acetylene Torch

In the forties Bill turned away from the drawings of lower-middle-class life and the chronicle of his small fry and began creating symbolical drawings influenced by both Picasso and the controversial psychiatric theorist Wilhelm Reich. Bill became both a patient and a disciple of Reich's and later illustrated a small book of his entitled *Listen, Little Man!* The drawings of this period, many of which are collected in *The Lonely Ones* and *Persistent Faces,* are in my opinion among the most satisfying of Bill's works. As character studies, they are both wider-ranging and more penetrating than any attempted by Leonardo da Vinci or Hogarth.

Bill is a man of great warmth and curiosity. His conversational style is direct and sometimes as innocent as a child's. Over his long career with this magazine, he has met with the editors Ross and Shawn on only two occasions. In each instance he expressed anger at what he felt was unfair treatment by the then head of the make-up department, Carmine

Peppe. It was and remains his conviction that Carmine disliked his work, and when he couldn't keep it out of the magazine altogether, he deliberately buried it in the back of the book. Bill complained often to Jim Geraghty about this, as he did to me. Bill once asked Jim if he "bitched more than anyone else." And Jim replied, "Bill, you bitch more than everyone else." I was sure Bill was wrong about Carmine's dislike of his work, but I could never convince Bill. Geraghty's unpublished notes reveal that we were both wrong. Steig's nemesis was not Carmine Peppe but Rea Irvin. Notes from Geraghty and also Ross and Katharine White make it clear that Irvin's continued reservations about Steig's drawings eventually led to his work being routed around the art meeting and handled directly through Ross's office. As a consequence Steig was always the last one to learn the result of the weekly meetings. It was this curious and persistent delay that first ignited his suspicions.

Bill's work has gone through almost as many phases as that of his idol, Picasso. The most important shift, in my opinion, came in the sixties and was inspired by a remark made by his son, the jazz flutist Jeremy Steig. Glancing at some of his father's sketches, Jeremy suggested that they would be improved if Bill stopped presketching in pencil and worked directly in ink. Bill accepted the challenge and threw away his pencils. The decision seems to have given him access to new reservoirs of energy and inventiveness from which he continues to create work of remarkable freshness. Such a move is unusual. Only a few artists—Al Ross, Don Reilly, and Ed Sorel come to mind—have the confidence to work with such directness.

Dutiful Son

Academician

Intellectual's Woman

Big City at Night

From his first carefully rendered covers of the thirties to the experimental watercolors of the eighties and nineties, **Bill** has been a resourceful colorist. This, combined with his unsurpassed skills as a writer, has made him an outstanding creator of books for children. Oddly enough, he claims to dislike using color—that is, he dislikes using it in the restrictive way required by book illustration. What he does love to do is to take a stack of old black-and-white drawings and color them in, with no worry about consistency, verisimilitude, or the problems of mechanical reproduction. The results are **Bill Steig** at his most satisfying. Only Picasso has been as successful at relearning as an adult the joyful abandon experienced by a child playing with crayons.

Mrs. Dixon loved cats.

A LA RECHERCHE DU TEMPS PERDU

Some European friends came to visit.

Papa was an expert rower.

SCENES FROM THE THOUSAND AND ONE NIGHTS

Pretending to be asleep, King Massoudah overhears talk about his wife's infidelity.

Sindbad is carried into the sky on the one day that the men of a certain land have wings.

Although the magazine had experimented with color in the twenties, Bob was the first editor to use it regularly. He used it to highlight pieces and occasionally to brighten "Goings On." He never used it in the cartoons (a policy Tina Brown has continued). What Bob did do was increase the use of colored spreads by Roz Chast, Michael Crawford, Glen Baxter, John Walker, and others. The first spread we ran in color was by William Steig. Seeing his *New Yorker* work in color seems to have inspired him, and over the next five years we purchased so many color pieces that we have yet to run them all. I often regret that color was not available when we were running some of Saul Steinberg's great sequences; although they appeared in the magazine in black and white, the originals were in magnificent color.

A two-page color spread by Rea Irvin from the issue dated December 12, 1925

The Maharajah of Puttyput receives a Christmas necktie from the Queen

Bob's search for new cover people bore early fruit. Two young artists quickly struck his fancy: the painter Bob Knox, who shared Bob's taste for visual puns, and Kathy Young, a young woman whose work I discovered among the portfolios that are dropped off every week. A third artist, whose appetite for outrageous puns seemed to surpass even Bob's, surfaced in one of my weekly siftings of the unsolicited mail. His name is John O'Brien. Although John had published a few cartoons elsewhere, he was supporting himself, at least during the winter months, as an illustrator of children's books. John spends his summers at the Jersey shore, where he is a senior lifeguard by day and a banjo player in a sing-along band by night.

I should also mention the work of a remarkable young artist from Belgium named Benoît van Innis. Benoît was brought to my attention by Rochelle Udell, who had seen his portfolio over at Condé Nast. Benoît's elegantly surrealistic style was right up Bob's alley, and he quickly became a regular contributor of both covers and spreads.

Feb. 6, 1989 · THE NEW YORKER · Price $1.75

THE FLAT TIRE

Handelsman
AFTER UTAMARO

June 26, 1989 · THE NEW YORKER · Price $1.75

Westman

Oct. 23, 1989 · THE NEW YORKER · Price $1.75

The difference between Bob's taste and Shawn's was a bonanza for some artists and a disaster for others. For the cartoonists, Bob's decision to run humor on the cover was a boon, and many of those who had seldom done covers before, including Bud Handelsman, Bob Mankoff, Roz Chast, Danny Shanahan, and myself, began to appear regularly, along with more familiar cartoonists like Ed Koren, George Booth, Ronald Searle, Don Reilly, and André François. The artists, however, who had been providing the quieter covers that Shawn favored were struggling. A few, notably Susan Davis, Gretchen Dow Simpson, and particularly Barbara Westman, were able to retool and provide material to Bob's liking, but artists like Lonnie Sue Johnson, Charlie Martin, Arthur Getz, and Robert Tallon seemed unable to adjust to Bob's taste.

Self-portrait by Art Spiegelman

Self-portrait by Lari Pittman

Self-portrait by Hunt Slonem

As color appeared more frequently, so did letters from old readers, who once again complained that standards were collapsing. In fact, as previously noted, *The New Yorker*, under Harold Ross and Rea Irvin, had used color as early as 1925. The truth is, almost all of Bob's innovations had solid precedents. Eustace Tilley had been a leading player in the illustrations accompanying Corey Ford's facetious history of the magazine, which ran in 1925 and 1926. Shawn had run photographs, and the celebrity portraits in "Goings On About Town" had been foreshadowed in the twenties by features created by Hans Stengel and Ralph Barton.

AS THEIR EYES MET FOR THAT VERY FIRST
TIME, RACHEL FELT HER WHOLE BEING
BECOME CONSUMED WITH ALMOST
TOTAL INDIFFERENCE.

TIME SEEMED TO STAND STILL.

EDGAR BEGAN TO FIND THE TENSION UNBEARABLE. HE
LOOKED IMPLORINGLY AT RACHEL AND STAMMERED,
"MAKE THINE INNERMOST DESIRES
KNOWN TO ME, MY DEAR."

ACCORDINGLY, RACHEL OBLIGED.

Take cab direct to Grand Central Station. Purchase ticket for first available train. Board same.

Glen Baxter

For most of its history the meaning of a closed door at *The New Yorker* was as clear as hanging a "Do Not Disturb" sign on the doorknob. To reach the person on the other side, a knock was considered as intrusive as a fireman's ax. Interoffice memos and circulating proofs were quietly slipped under the door, and more personal communications were initiated with a discreet message left at the switchboard. These formalities, ritualized over the magazine's first sixty years, quickly melted away under the influence of Bob Gottlieb's direct, unbuttoned style. Bob never wore a tie and he only closed his office door during fire drills. As a result, everyone at the magazine quickly gained a sense of Bob's special taste in interior decoration. He couldn't resist anything truly awful: gold-painted seashells, paintings on black velvet, lamps that would have made George Price blush. The most arresting pieces in his office were the self-framed paint-by-numbers pictures. (These collections were purely recreational and were not reflected in Bob's choice of material for the magazine.) Bob's enthusiasms were contagious, and each week fresh additions to his collection were offered by staff members, who had plucked them from suburban tag sales. The most memorable gift was a piece of found art retrieved from an alley in Greenwich Village. It was a large blowup of a photograph of Joan Crawford, handtinted, and pasted to a three-by-four-foot piece of corrugated cardboard. To complete the effect, cheap black lace was pasted around the photo as a kind of veil. Under this portrait, an icon of trash culture, Bob and I met every week for most of our years together, to select cartoons and covers for what was still considered one of the most sophisticated magazines in the world.

The small, decorative drawings that for most of our history have been sprinkled across the magazine's pages are called "spots." Traditionally, they have performed three important functions. For the make-up department, they were an indispensable tool for filling out short copy. ("Newsbreaks" often served the same function.)

For the reader they provided an opportunity to rest the eye—a small oasis in the drifting sands of text. They also provided an entry-level opportunity for many of the magazine's artists. George Price, James Thurber, Gretchen Dow Simpson, Charles Saxon, Henry Martin, and James Stevenson are

just a few of the cartoonists and cover artists who debuted here as producers of spot drawings.

As a consequence of the magazine's dramatically expanded graphic vocabulary under Bob Gottlieb and Tina Brown, the spot drawing is now just one of many options available to the design staff. The spots appearing today have been commissioned by head designer Caroline Mailhot to work within something unknown to the earlier magazine: a coherent design philosophy.

Joe Davis

Having said that, one can regret the passing of a tradition that brought delight to several generations of readers. The now retired spot bank contained thousands of drawings—many dating back to the twenties and thirties. Favorites reappeared regularly, and coming across them in our pages was, for many readers, like unexpectedly bumping into old friends.

J. Oliver

J.J.S.

weil

LB

I van Rynbach

Richard Edes Harrison

THE NEW YORKER
THE TALK OF THE TOWN

Notes and Comment

ADDERS of insult to injury are the department stores which pick out zero days for display, ing one-piece bathing suits in windows. We rather suspect connivance with Florida chambers of commerce, ever alert to proselytize in the frigid

northlands. If you happen to take your winter straight, it is no fun to skid, half dead with cold, around an icy Fifth Avenue corner, only to have a papier-mâché diving girl thrown up in your chapped face.

EVIDENCE that the country is in its usual state of normalcy in the reports that Mr. Chaplin's films are being barred here and there. This is usual. Our quick guess is that the emotions of the persons instituting the censorship are as follows: 30 per cent for putting Mr. Chaplin off the screen as a possible menace, 70 per cent for putting themselves, in print, plainly On the Side of Right.

TWO EVIDENCES that the Tunney influence is striking at the vitals of national ignorance have

we startled between the covers of the *Mercury*. Drawn thus suddenly from the green paths of erudition, his interest in us as a possible fare was only so-so. The second evidence was reported by a publisher, who said a policeman in full uniform paid a visit to the publishing house to ask for a copy of rules governing auction bridge.

WE CONTINUE to hear that Mr. William Randolph Hearst appears determined to embellish California with an ancient Cistercian cloister at the expense of Segovia, Spain, and the Segovian natives appear to be howling at Mr. Hearst, declaring that he has no right to take their cloister even though he has paid for it. The poor Segovians are wasting their breath. At the risk of being funny, we wish to point out that large fractions of the people of America have been howling at Mr. Hearst for more than a generation without influencing him perceptibly.

UNFORTUNATELY, on nice bright days pessimism sometimes loses much of its appeal, and one is assailed by pleasant thoughts in spite of onrself. We could not avoid regarding with delight and enthusiasm, after a snowfall, the roof-tops lower than our own. Everybody (unless he be very rich) has enjoyed the pleasure of going out into the woods in the morning and seeing in the snow the tracks of the invisible wild things that have gamboled there. So with the roof-tops. No one ever sees anybody on roofs in winter,

yet the snow is inevitably marked with tracks a day or so after it has fallen. The conclusion, we suppose, is that we're all animals anyway.

BROADWAY has its moments of glamorous beauty when it shines forth, an amazing spectacle of foolish bright existence, but for every one of

these moments there are long dull hours of the day and night when it is as tawdry as Coney at its worst.

The latest side-show is the Lucky Strike exhibit at Forty-fifth Street, where cigarettes are manufactured (step up, folks) under the horny gaze of a multitude who seem to have come straight from the boardwalk at Atlantic City. Shops along the highway are unnecessarily garish. There is an unnecessary amount of noise and pushing. Faces, so it seems, are unnecessarily vulgar. And if ever, in a might mood, you should want to look man's work and despair, stroll do Broadway about three in the mor when the lights are gone and the d street sprawls slant-wise acro town in all the ugly mean disuse.

Rosa Lewis

IT SEEMS that Mrs. known somewhat s the Queen of Cooks, sad-faced old preterists gathering each day at Ritz to recall the me dinners served in th...

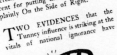

turned up within the week. One was the chauffeur of a parked taxi, whom

THE NEW YORKER
THE TALK OF THE TOWN

Notes and Comment

NOT the least amusing thing about the new Garden is the character of the ticket-takers Tex Rickard has put at the doors. They are tough, tout-like, heavy-jowled, and heavy-bellied—the Irish appendage of the sporting arena since time immemorial. They are exactly like the political attendants one sees in the court-house except that instead of being unnecessarily disagreeable they are busy politely taking tickets.

THE statement by Mr. Harvie, head of the Association of Trolley Cars, to the effect that the motor bus is not a competitor of the trolley but an adjunct, is a wonderful thing. It has strengthened the opinion we hold as a psychologist and biologist that man always believes what he wants to believe, an opinion which has helped us to understand why prohibitionists say prohibition is a success.

IF it be a privilege to dress shop windows, why then it follows that the man whose privilege it is to dress the

front window of the Flatiron Building is the most blessed of men. His creations face Broadway, Fifth Avenue, and Twenty-third Street. Nevertheless, blessed though he is, if we ever meet him we will tell him out and out

that nine days out of ten his window is the dullest in all New York.

WE think that the drive to make New York the art center of the world, which is to start February tenth, has an excellent chance of succeeding. While feeling in our hearts that art is certainly for art's sake, we are cynical enough, looking back at Athens, Rome, Alexandria, Venice, Florence, and the like, to believe that the art center is always where the most money is.

WE always try to print some small fruit of our unwearied imagination each week for the benefit of the tired business man. This week it

is our belief that the perfumer who first hits on the idea of getting four hundred members of the Yale, Harvard, and Princeton Clubs to endorse the taste of a lipstick will make a fortune.

DURING one of the frightfully cold, windy days of the recent cold snap we saw Ina Claire, lovely actress, on the street. It is not our wish or our intention to make an enemy of her press agent—but, like everybody else, she had a red nose.

ACCORDING to the researches of social scientists, the geographical society center of New York has moved

northward two blocks in one year. We have an unworthy suspicion that it must have gone on a Madison Avenue car.

The Week

FORMER Kaiser Wilhelm celebrates his sixty-seventh birthday, elated over prospect of regaining his

fortune, and funeral services are held for Cardinal Mercier. Colonel Mitchell submits resignation when President approves court martial findings and Senate votes for U. S. adherence to World Court. Elihu Root denounces agricultural bloc as attempt at minority rule and Stock Exchange investigates practice of selling only non-voting stock in corporations to public. Miss Helen Wills meets success in her first tennis tournaments abroad and Big Bill Tilden makes his debut as a professional actor. It is announced that this country now has 100,000 garages and Henry Ford deplores the passing of the old-fashioned barn dance. Turkish Government establishes oil monopoly and Standard Oil Company of California is incorporated for $1,500,000,000. Commissioner McLaughlin defends police raids without warrants and patrolman is found guilty of first degree murder for shooting citizen who complained about him. Bishop sees world in throes of religious re-birth and representa-

Few artists have done more to establish the tone of *The New Yorker* than Otto Soglow, who joined the magazine in 1925 and retired in 1974. Over his career he produced thousands of spot drawings and hundreds of cartoons, including the wildly successful "Little King" series, which became both a syndicated cartoon and an animated feature. His most distinctive contribution were the hundreds of small drawings he produced weekly for more than forty-five years for the "Talk of the Town" section.

Otto was a short man with a large head, and wore a stoic expression that always reminded me of Buster Keaton. I first met him at a National Cartoonists Society dinner, where he was the featured performer in a variety of skits which provided the evening's entertainment. He appeared onstage before the wildly enthusiastic crowd dressed in a long blond wig and, accompanied by the music from *Scheherazade*, did his own version of "the dance of the seven veils." By the time the seventh veil fell, Otto was stark naked. He raced

offstage to the cheers of the audience, then standing on its feet. This memory was in my mind in 1973, when, after I became art editor, Otto appeared in our outer office to prepare his weekly batch of drawings for the "Talk of the Town" pages. The man who walked into my office that day approached his job not with the wild abandon of the ecdysiast but with the quiet competence of a CPA. He arrived, said hello, hung up his hat, and sat down on a small worktable in the outer office. I handed him a folder of "Talk" pieces, prepared by

THE NEW YORKER

THE TALK OF THE TOWN

Notes and Comment

OUR ghastliness prize for the week ending September 22nd goes to the Chiclet people, who do their little things up in stuff called Sylphrap. There is enough horror in the world without bringing Sylphrap into it. Even if we were sure that sylphs wore cellophane pants, we couldn't help dividing the word the way it first seemed natural to divide it: syl-phrap. Phrap for short.

HAVING awarded ghastliness honors to Chiclets, we are glad to bestow Meanest Dog of Show to Circuit Judge Leslie A. Bruce, of Missouri.

Judge Bruce discovered, by reading the papers, that two couples whose divorce decrees he had granted had remarried—each man marrying the other's former wife. This arrangement, which was not only legal but presumably entirely satisfactory to the four people, failed to satisfy Judge Bruce; he said it must have indicated collusion, and forthwith annulled the divorces, which made the old marriage ties binding again after an unwittingly adulterous interlude. This may have been sense of duty on the Judge's part; but it smacks more of that peculiar brand of righteous indignation which borders so perilously on envy.

WE see the cranberry-pickers are striking for better working conditions. Maybe the ground is too boggy.

THERE is said to be a fine cure now for agranulocytosis (death of white corpuscles). There is said, also, to exist a substance in one's kidneys which, if there's enough of it, will provide immunity from cancer. The cause

of leukemia in chickens has been discovered, and a serum is being developed for infantile paralysis. All these discoveries in the field of medicine give us a cheery feeling of progress; that is, they would give us a cheery feeling of progress if we thought any corresponding improvement was noticeable in the field of diagnosis—or what we call "going to the doctor." After all, the remedy for agranulocytosis is useful only if one's physician manages to discover, by showing a little interest, that you have agranulocytosis. Yet any adult knows that going to the doctor is still pretty much where it was: the doctor mulls over his records, places a wooden paddle on your tongue, and makes a dirty crack about your tonsils. And there are always just enough patients who feel bad but *haven't* got agranulocytosis, so that he gets away with it.

IN cubicle of kitchen at the midnight hour, we filch cheese from the icebox to spread on crackers from the shelf; and when we are done, and have gathered up the crumbs and bits of foil, we press the pedal on the garbage pail and the lid opens with the simplest yet most magical of motions. This foot-operated garbage lid, which has saved so many million stoopings of so many tired houseworkers, sometimes seems the great monument to native ingenuity. A garbage-pail lid responding to

toe pressure is more than a mere labor-saving motion, it is a soul-satisfying one. We grow accustomed to it; but it is spectacular to anyone witnessing it for the first time. Someone who lives near us has been telling us of a Frenchwoman, a lady of distinguished ancestry, who visited here during August

and was dutifully shown skyscraper cathedrals, cocktail bars, vehicular tunnels, and other evidences of our national greatness. She was politely unimpressed, till she chanced into her host's kitchen one morning and observed the garbage pail in action. Last week she returned to France, a genuine American garbage pail the only trophy of her trip to the new world.

GARBAGE disposal is a livelier experience at sea than on land, even granting the satisfactions of the pedal pail. In a ship over whose garbage we once presided in a minor capacity, the chute was the headquarters for half the gulls in the North Pacific, and we

their patron saint, particularly on days following meat stew. Houses are too steady for proper disposal, and there are no birds on waiting wings.

THERE was a dreary, unsubstantial-looking gentleman fumbling around our office this morning, complaining about his relations with the federal government. It seems he had to pay some back income taxes, and the thing festering in his mind was that he was required to pay it *plus six-per-cent interest*. "Try and get six-per-cent interest from anybody, these days," he murmured, biting off pieces of our rubber typewriter cover and spitting them out thoughtfully onto the floor. "Six per cent has gone the way of pug dogs and diabolo—it's out! There's a new deal, and six per cent isn't mentioned in it—except when the Treasury Department collects back taxes. The government pays about three and a quarter per cent on its new Liberties, and much less on short-term loans. I'm not usually a complaining man," he said, "but con-

William Shawn's office, and a list indicating which ones he should illustrate. Otto accepted this silently, seated himself at the worktable, put on his glasses, and began to read. After thirty minutes or so, he put aside the copy and began to sketch in pencil on illustration board. He never made preliminary sketches either for me or for himself. After completing the pencil drawing, he carefully inked

in the finishes with a pen he had brought with him. After the ink dried, he cleaned the drawings with a rubber eraser, placed them in the folio along with the appropriate "Talk" pieces, handed the folio back to me, put on his hat, shook my hand, and left. I don't remember ever receiving a drawing that was unpublishable or required correction. His deceptively simple but incisive

sketches were the perfect garnish to the quiet humor of the "Talk" section—in those days, a mild smorgasbord of commentary and reflection. After Soglow retired, Mr. Shawn and I spent many fruitless hours trying to find a replacement. In the end we gave up. Otto's drawings, like his striptease, required no encore.

Unsolicited cartoons are dumped each week into the so-called slush box. The item in question is a gray-painted wooden box, approximately two feet square and ten inches deep. Except for the coffeepot I had installed for the use of contract artists in 1975, it is the only artifact from the regime of Shawn and Gottlieb which remains in use in the art department today. I offered it to the Smithsonian when we moved from 25 West Forty-third Street, but they chose instead the cot on which Calvin Trillin used to take his afternoon naps and the make-up department's obsolete equipment.

The furor over the ownership of the Thurber wall inspired many staff members to create faux Thurbers on the walls of empty offices. Here I am with fact editor, now theatre critic, Nancy Franklin.

On February 22, 1991, *The New Yorker* moved from the north side of Forty-third Street to new premises on the south side of Forty-third Street. Having begun life in 1925 at Forty-fifth Street, we were moving southward at a steady speed—about a block every two decades. At this rate, we should be celebrating, someone calculated, our 275th anniversary in the Empire State Building. Although some felt sentimental about leaving the old premises, as we began to clear out files and move furniture, it became apparent to staffers what many had long suspected: the *New Yorker* offices had deteriorated from charmingly shabby to hazardously shabby. Had *The New Yorker* been a delicatessen, it would have been condemned years earlier.

One aspect of this move that seemed to catch the public's attention was the removal of the so-called Thurber wall. The wall was actually a small group of sketches including some of Thurber's favorite subjects: football players, implacable women, downtrodden men, a dying tree or two, and a dog. The work also includes a very convincing self-portrait. Thurber made these sketches in the thirties, and up to the present time they were really visible only to those fortunate enough to occupy his former office. The magazine's CEO, Steve Florio, decided that the drawings were one of *The New Yorker*'s treasures, and had the wall supporting the drawings cut out and removed to be rehung in a more public space on the new premises. When the owners read about this plan in *The New York Times*, they decided, with some justification, that since the walls were part of their building, the drawings were part of *their* heritage. After considerable posturing on both sides, the drawings were reunited in a glass-covered case outside the current art department on the sixteenth floor. *The New Yorker*'s former landlord, not to be entirely left out, installed a brass plaque in the entrance way listing important *New Yorker* contributors whose talents had flourished upon his premises.

If *The New Yorker*'s offices on the north side of Forty-third Street can be described as an ill-kept rabbit warren, the new premises, on the south side of the street, suggest the architectural ambitions of Albert Speer and the Third Reich. The narrow, tangled corridors have been replaced with vast, well-lit freeways, and the drab, dun-colored walls are now a Bauhaus white, regularly scoured and retouched. The main architectural feature on the editorial floors (the baronial splendor of the business department is the subject of a separate book) is what is often described as a late-Mussolini staircase leading from the art department, on the sixteenth floor, to the editor's office, on the seventeenth floor. The upper landing leads into a plaza area larger than most New York City nightclubs. In an attempt to put this space to good use, managing editor Chip McGrath and art critic Adam Gopnik once gave a memorable exhibition of one-on-one Rollerblade hockey. (Shortly after Tina Brown became editor, the space was reorganized into workstations for the design department and for various editorial assistants.)

Bob, who seized any opportunity to encourage fraternization among the staff, punctuated the halls with coffee stations. He also added a canteen on the north side of the seventeenth floor, including soda and snack machines, a microwave oven, and a color television set. Booths along the windows offered the staff an opportunity to enjoy the view along with lunch. The view, unfortunately, was directly into *The New Yorker*'s old offices, which were still empty. Most people preferred to work the *Times* crossword puzzle during lunch or watch television.

In terms of the art department, the new premises resulted in three significant changes. The art vault, where covers and purchased drawings are stored, is now across the corridor, rather than two floors away. Secondly, I would now walk up one flight of stairs to the art meeting rather than down one flight of stairs. And thirdly, my unparalleled view of the Chrysler Building was replaced by an unparalleled view of the Empire State Building.

Louis Rojas, caretaker of *The New Yorker* archives, in the basement at 25 West Forty-third Street

When I first was given office space at the magazine, I, like most others on the premises, spent most of my time quietly working with the door closed. Even innocent conversation around the watercooler was discouraged, and if one could combine a trip to the men's room with a trip out to lunch, one would have saved oneself a great deal of potential embarrassment. This meant that unless you had an immersion heater in your office, you went for long stretches without either coffee or tea. I don't think any of us realized how crippling this deprivation was until Bob Gottlieb took over as editor. One of Bob's first moves was to install coffee stations, several on each floor. This immediately changed the pace of life at *The New Yorker*. Bob, unlike Ross or Shawn, encouraged fraternization among staff members, and the coffee stations soon became the social hub of the magazine. If one were to write the history of *The New Yorker* from a pharmacological point of view, I think it would be fair to say that for the first sixty years it ran on alcohol, under Bob Gottlieb it switched to caffeine, and under Tina Brown (with the addition of Art Spiegelman and Françoise Mouly) it seems to be now running on nicotine.

In the fall of '91 *The New Yorker* was approached by a large Japanese advertising agency to participate in a weeklong multimedia seminar, in Tokyo, on the subject of art in the cities. *The New Yorker* was asked to organize a small show of covers relating to New York as a background for the roundtable and featured seminars. Speakers from both countries would discuss topics related to both art and city life. I was invited to participate, and my wife and I made plans for a trip to Japan. In early spring, the plans were changed and several editorial people, including me, were disinvited. When I put this together with what seemed, to me, a shift in Bob Gottlieb's usually ebullient manner, I began to suspect that something was in the wind. Rumors had been circulating that Newhouse was dissatisfied with Bob's performance, but rumors now were as common around *The New Yorker* as they are around Wall Street or Washington, D.C. On the thirtieth of June, 1992, while Bob was in Japan, S. I. Newhouse announced that he would in fact be replaced by the high-profile, high-voltage editor of *Vanity Fair*, Tina Brown.

On the surface, it would be hard to imagine editorial styles more dissimilar than Robert Gottlieb's and William Shawn's. At the same time, they shared some essential characteristics: neither knew how to delegate authority; both were workaholics. Most importantly, both viewed the magazine as a forum for its contributors and not as a soapbox for the views of either the editor or the publisher.

Bob had kept his promise to bring evolutionary, not revolutionary, change to *The New Yorker*. He had brought to the magazine an impressive group of new artists and writers. The changes he made in the art department are particularly worth noting. He expanded the editorial use of color, he regularly used photography, he re-created the "Goings On" section as an editorial feature and created an illustration department for this purpose. Certainly the increasing use of commissioned illustrations, which had been a feature of Ross's *New Yorker*, was one of Bob's most important legacies in the art area to the next editor of the magazine.

Bob had often been quoted as saying he had three ambitions in life: to run a major publishing house—and, of course, he had been editor in chief at Knopf; to be involved in the ballet—and he had been on the board of the New York City Ballet; and, finally, to be editor of *The New Yorker* magazine. As editor here, Bob managed to combine the high spirits and sense of adventure that characterized Ross's *New Yorker* with the serious journalistic purposes of Shawn's magazine. The discussions between Newhouse and Gottlieb which preceded his resignation were candidly reported in a memo distributed to the staff. It was clear that Bob had gone as far as he was prepared to go; to go further, Newhouse needed a new editor, and he chose Tina Brown.

Although the announcement of Bob's replacement was made in June, Tina did not actually assume control of the magazine until September. The intervening months had an odd, surreal quality. Bob, of course, had known what was coming, and though he could not have been happy about leaving, there was also a noticeable relaxation in his manner that suggested some level of relief. Bob even threw a farewell party for the staff at the home of his friend Paul Taylor and invited me to bring along my jazz band.

While Tina began to assemble her new team, Bob and I continued to meet regularly on Tuesday afternoons to purchase cartoons and schedule covers. (Tina wanted her first official issue, October 5, to have a cover of her own choice, so we only scheduled up to that date.) Bob's established routine with Rochelle Udell and Ingrid Sischy also continued into the fall.

A Tuesday afternoon art meeting with Tina Brown and Rick Hertzberg

Tina, her managing editor, Pam McCarthy, and the other new members of Tina's skeleton staff set up their offices in a remote corner of the sixteenth floor, which had been set aside for the accounting department. (The accounting department had since moved to Condé Nast.) This unused space had become a dumping ground for battered furniture, storage files, and back issues—the flotsam and jetsam of corporate life. Compared to the rest of the premises, it looked like the South Bronx, but as the staging area for Tina's new *New Yorker,* it was dubbed by the staff the Manhattan Project.

After settling in, Tina brought over an intense, direct young woman named Maurie Perl to handle the media's interest in the transition. Paparazzi stalked Tina in the lobby, and one freelance photographer bluffed his way onto the premises to surreptitiously photograph Tina's first meeting with the artists. (Five years earlier another photographer had ambushed Shawn and Gottlieb lunching at the Algonquin.)

Although bringing out the weekly issue remained the first priority, there seemed to be plenty of time left over to speculate on Tina's intentions. Her two published books, *Life as a Party* and *Loose Talk*, collections of profiles and occasional journalism, were passed around, and her professional résumé hung in many offices next to the editorial phone list.

Tina's career had started fast, and seems to have accelerated. She was winning awards as a journalist in London twenty years ago. In 1978 her work for *Punch* and *The Sunday Telegraph Magazine* earned her an award as Young Journalist of the Year. From 1979 to 1983 Tina edited *Tatler*, which under her guidance saw its circulation rise by 300 percent. Her success at *Vanity Fair*, including numerous magazine awards, was well known, but was there any common ground between *The New Yorker*'s tradition of sober, reflective journalism and the eye-popping, freewheeling spirit of *Vanity Fair*?

Tina Brown decided that there was, and reached back beyond her predecessors, Bob Gottlieb and William Shawn, to find it. The inspiration for her *New Yorker*, she announced in a meeting with the staff, would be Harold Ross, and his *New Yorker*. Certainly the earlier magazine had a rough-and-ready, let's-try-anything quality, which appealed to Tina's sense of adventure. (This air of improvisation probably was as much a result of a lack of cash as an excess of inspiration.) In any case, the early *New Yorker* did provide a precedent for many of Tina's graphic innovations: an increased number of illustrated department heads, expanded illustration, graphic reportage, more imaginative layouts, and a kind of freedom in the cartoons that hadn't been seen since the salad days of Peter Arno. Tina refused "to regard *The New Yorker* as a stuffed bird, of which I am the curator." After weekends spent examining issues from the magazine's first decade, she decided that Ross's magazine, under Irvin, had been "more than modern, it was cutting edge."

Throughout July and August, while the current *New Yorker* was running at half-speed, Tina was working with two young designers—Caroline Mailhot and Wynn Dan—to re-create the magazine in the spirit of Harold Ross. Heads and margins were rescaled, a more flexible grid was created for the text, and new department heads were created. (Over the years most of the heads created by Rea Irvin had been retired.) "Notes and Comment" was separated from "Talk" and moved to the front of the book. "Critics" were herded together in the rear of the magazine, which now ended with "Shouts and Murmurs" (Alexander Woollcott's original column).

"I'd like to go back and change my shirt."

"Please continue talking, Briggs. I have to keep moving lest I suffocate and die."

"For some reason, we weren't appealing enough to those awful little bastards everyone hates."

Tina well understood the importance of the cartoonists to the magazine, and at one of our first meetings she asked me to arrange a meeting with them as soon as possible. It turned out to be a large gathering, standing-room-only, and it was held in one of *The New Yorker*'s small conference rooms. Addressing the artists, Tina expressed her desire for cutting-edge humor and extreme timeliness. Sex was definitely in, and whimsy and puns were definitely out. She also made it clear that in terms of both drawings and captions, traditional community standards would be considered only one of several possible options. Franker language and more explicit drawing were acceptable if they sharpened the joke. Tina's remarks were to the point, and during the question and answer period her responses were both sharp and funny. The artists emerged from these meetings reassured and with their spirits considerably buoyed.

"Those were the days, my friend, We thought they'd never end."

"Still, the Trojan War might well have gone the other way if the Greeks had excluded gays from their armed forces."

THE GRAND TETONS EN BUSTIER

CROSSED PATHS
Chagall Meets Toscanini

"I do hope you'll excuse the formality of the clamps."

"Food as a metaphor for love? Again?"

"I know what women want. Her lawyer told me."

"Sweetie, show the Hazlitts the watercolors
you made in jail."

"Its DNA is consistent with meat loaf."

"No, Thursday's out. How about never—is never
good for you?"

It was evident from the beginning that Tina's new *New Yorker* would require more art and more kinds of art than we'd ever run before. Since we would now be commissioning much of this material, I felt free to reach out to artists I admired but had been reluctant to speak to earlier. I quickly worked my way through my own Rolodex and Rolodexes of several friends, including Steve Heller at *The New York Times*, and created a small list of artists whose work I felt would fit comfortably into Tina's magazine. These included Sue Coe, Arnold Roth, Paul Davis, Maurice Sendak, Bruce McCall, Jules Feiffer, and Red Grooms.

While Caroline and Wynn and their associates were poring over their light tables back in the Manhattan Project, Tina was soliciting suggestions from the other members of the staff, among them Chip McGrath, Roger Angell, Ren Weschler (Ren was both a friend and admirer of Art Spiegelman and was the one who brought Tina and Art together), Adam Gopnik, illustration editor Chris Curry, and myself. Up to this point, Tina's intention had been to stick with *The New Yorker*'s traditional black-and-white format. However, a package she received from Chris Curry while she was vacationing out in Quogue changed her mind.

Chris had put together two portfolios of color samples, one of caricature and portraits, and one of spots and illustrations. She suggested that these be used to enliven the "Goings On" section, for which she had been supplying illustrations for the past three years. Tina's response was enthusiastic. "I saw," she said later, "that my black-and-white concept was not pure; it was funereal."

Tina was understandably anxious to make a bit of a splash with her first cover. She hoped for one that would convey the wit and energy of Ross's magazine in a manner that was both contemporary and topical. Work was solicited from several artists, and the most promising I forwarded to Tina, who was at that time staying with her family at a dude ranch, the Spear-O-Wigwam Ranch in Sheridan, Wyoming. After putting her children to bed, Tina spread the work of the leading candidates out on her bunk. Tina's choice was Edward Sorel's sketch of a spike-haired punk disdainfully surveying the glorious fall foliage as he rolled through Central Park in a horse-drawn carriage.

Ed's finished piece was even more successful than the sketch, and the public response to it fulfilled Tina's high expectations. For years people had been calling *The New Yorker* to ask for issue dates of Ed Sorel covers, which in fact had appeared elsewhere; the assumption of course was, they *should* have appeared on *The New Yorker*. The quality and range of the work Ed has done for us since that first cover proves that they were right.

The seaweed on the shore cries out,
But only it knows what about.

The person who today is here
May by tomorrow disappear.

One cannot hope to end one's life
With nothing but a butter knife.

The widespread use of color in the magazine is perhaps the most obvious feature of Tina Brown's *New Yorker*. This commitment to color has been a boon not only to a new generation of illustrators now appearing in our pages but to the magazine's established cartoonists as well. The artists were encouraged to produce color material to suit a new one-column format, as well as to produce spreads and single-page features. Along with new artists like Steve Brodner, Bill Griffith, and Barry Blitt, familiar contributors such as Roz Chast, Michael Crawford, and Bill Steig have taken advantage of this opportunity to add some new arrows to their quivers.

Having committed herself to color, Tina's next and most revealing decision was to have a maquette of each week's issue in the office of Caroline Mailhot to help her in laying out the issue. This essentially is the magazine itself, each page scaled down to three by four inches and laid out in sequence. Working from this, Tina was able to pace the flow of color pieces through the magazine. This cinematic approach to each week's issue is undoubtedly responsible for the heightened cadence of the new *New Yorker*. It's also worth noting that Tina herself grew up in a film culture, her father having been a film producer.

"The Hard Nut" at the Next Wave Festival

In 1925 Harold Ross's magazine carried so much art and the art was so well received that one critic described it as the best magazine in the world for people who cannot read. In 1995 Tina Brown's *New Yorker*, though definitely a magazine for people who *can* read, rivals Ross's in the range, brilliance, and stylistic diversity of its art. Caricatures, spots, satiric features, strips, illustrations, as well as cartoons were regularly featured in the twenties, but in some areas she has even outpaced her model. One of Tina's most discussed innovations has been to encourage artists to use the covers as a kind of editorial platform for deeply felt personal statements. (The "Notes and Comment" section has traditionally been available for writers in much the same way.) Art Spiegelman's "Valentine's Day" cover is just the most notorious example of this trend, but there have been others, including Josh Gosfield's moving tribute to Malcolm X and Judith Schaechter's stained-glass window, entitled "Night Flower," which was designed as an homage to Sylvia Plath.

A JEW IN ROSTOCK
by Art Spiegelman

Shawn had occasionally run photographs and Bob had used them regularly, but until Tina hired Richard Avedon as a contributing photographer, photography had never been a regular feature at the magazine. Ironically, as more and more color appears in our pages, Avedon's stark black-and-white photographs have an impact that perhaps they would not have had at an earlier time. Although they occasionally accompany or amplify a text, most of them appear as freestanding editorial pieces. Avedon's range has broadened dramatically since Winthrop Sargeant profiled him as an innovative fashion photographer in *The New Yorker* dated November 8, 1958. Even so, Avedon's continuing ability to suggest what led up to and what might follow the pivotal moment caught on film is strikingly like the cartoonists' ability to freeze the decisive moment in their mini-dramas. Sargeant put it this way: "It is this power to induce the conviction that one is witnessing a crucial instant in the emotional life of the subject, and to stimulate curiosity as to what brought it about and what will ensue, that gives the Avedon photograph its peculiar distinction."

During this hectic transition period, confusion was sometimes compounded by miscommunication. Tina expressed to me an interest in running on a regular basis a series of artist's portfolios, which I understood to mean graphic work not created for publication but of sufficient narrative interest to merit space in the magazine. During the early fall I made several trips to galleries and studios and eventually assembled sample portfolios of half a dozen artists, only to discover upon presenting them that what Tina really had in mind was a kind of graphic reportage. This idea again was an echo of Ross's *New Yorker*, which regularly dispatched artists, including Reginald Marsh and Helen Hokinson, to cover events here in Manhattan. This seemed an assignment more appropriate to narrative or strip artists than the magazine's traditional gag cartoonists, and I suggested that we approach a few of the best known, including Art Spiegelman, Robert Crumb, and Ben Katchor. Tina, not for the last time, was way ahead of me. Art had already agreed to draw a piece on his scheduled trip to Rostock in connection with a German edition of his classic *Maus*. This turned out to be the perfect vehicle for *The New Yorker*'s first venture into this form of reportage.

Art's later contributions, a tribute to the late Harvey Kurtzman and a joint venture with Maurice Sendak, as well as the weekly strips recently featured in "Talk," suggest the flexibility and range of this combination of text and pictures.

**W. H. Auden, photographed by
Richard Avedon on St. Mark's Place in
New York City, 1960**

Anatomy of an ACTION THRILLER

The making of "CLEAR AND PRESENT DANGER"

by P. Plitt

Bigwigs

Among the four hundred cast and crew members were genuine military personnel, taking time from defending the country to appear as extras.

ARS LONGA VITA BREVIS

EXCELSIOR

BEAT IT

Saul Steinberg

MANHATTAN
Fame accosts Faulkner outside the Dakota, December, 1952.

Zelda and Scott Fitzgerald: He had a hard time depicting her. Love—and self-love—got in the way.

Although the magazine seems to pop and bubble with color, it was agreed that the cartoons themselves would remain black-and-white. Ross's often quoted remark "What's funny about red?" was in response to the suggestion that printing cartoons in color would in some way improve them. The continued unwillingness of Shawn, Gottlieb, and now Tina Brown to colorize the cartoons confirms the correctness of Ross's view.

On September 17, 1992, I sent a production report to Tina to tell her where we stood in terms of the art she had selected. At that point the October 5 cover by Ed Sorel had been separated and was at the printer. Robert Risko's "Trick or Treat" cover, scheduled for November 2, was also at the printer, as was Steinberg's Thanksgiving cover. Three other covers had been separated and were available standbys. Six more, including works by Red Grooms and Josh Gosfield's "Malcolm X" (originally purchased as an inside piece), were being proofed. In addition to these, we of course had dozens of covers in our existing inventory. Many of these previously purchased covers, by the way, later turned up in the magazine as full-color pages.

In the same memo I noted that five artists, Arnie Levin, Bud Handelsman, Arnold Roth, Jules Feiffer, and Gahan Wilson, were developing ideas for a proposed strip feature for "The Talk of the Town." Eventually over a dozen artists produced sketches for what we had envisioned as a continuing chronicle of Manhattan, a kind of weekly diary written and drawn by one artist. This feature never gelled in that form, but it did surface again in 1994, as a "Talk" feature done by various artists on a rotating basis, covering current events in the city.

"BRAM STOKER'S BAMBI"

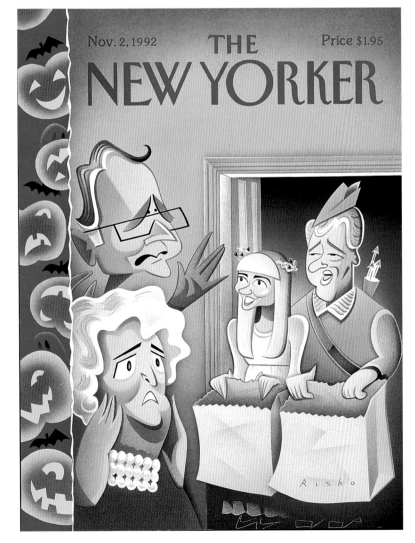

Nov. 2, 1992 THE NEW YORKER Price $1.95

Philip Burke

Geena Davis, Andy Garcia, and Dustin Hoffman in "Hero"

Jon Hendricks at Fat Tuesday's

The New Yorker had the good fortune to have been born during a particularly rich period in the history of caricature, and the early magazine published memorable work by the leading practitioners of the day. Miguel Covarrubias, though often identified with *Vanity Fair*, appeared regularly in our pages, as did the wonderfully gifted Ralph Barton. There were hardly enough outlets for the prolific Mr. Barton, and although he did memorable work for *The New Yorker*, his career was not as closely bound to the magazine as that of his colleague Al Frueh. Frueh's world was as gay and guileless as Barton's was astringent and angst-ridden. (Barton could draw the Marx Brothers in a way that suggested the Four Horsemen of the Apocalypse.) In addition to decorating the theatre section, caricatures regularly accompanied profiles, "A Reporter at Large," and "The Talk of the Town." Early features such as "Heroes of the Week" and "Gotham Gazette" were little more than excuses for these artists to display their virtuosity.

The cast of "Designing Women," left to right: Meshach Taylor, Jan Hooks, Dixie Carter, Judith Ivey, and Annie Potts

Edward R. Murrow

Al Frueh, who illustrated our theatre page from 1925 until his retirement in 1962, was our most prolific contributor, but William Cotton, Abe Birnbaum, and William Auerbach-Levy also produced distinguished work through the forties.

A shift in public taste after the war and William Shawn's preference for more literal portrait sketches diminished the importance of caricature to the magazine. This continued through the eighties, when, under Bob Gottlieb, caricature began reappearing. Tom Bloom, Michael Witte, and Robert deMichiell did notable work in the magazine's revamped "Goings On About Town" section, and caricature began to crop up throughout the magazine.

Under Tina Brown, caricature has roared back with a vengeance. Sly, bold, hilarious, and occasionally devastating work by Gerald Scarfe, Robert Risko, Philip Burke, and Ed Sorel now animates our pages much as it did in the twenties. Caricature has even spilled over to the outside of the magazine.

The public figures caricatured on recent covers have received an honor previously awarded to only Adolf Hitler and the victorious Allies during World War II.

ON THE WINGS OF DREAMS
Not a nightmare, but a nightfish, is what Helen Ford and Lulu McConnell are riding, full of fancy, through the melodious sequences of the musical comedy, "Peggy-Ann," at the Vanderbilt. The plot is the same as "Tillies's Nightmare," which adds to the easy grace of their passage o'er the waves.

"SERENA BLANDISH"
Here we have Ruth Gordon as the much too amiable young lady around whose inability to get a husband the comedy at the Morosco revolves.

Richard L. Simon

M. Lincoln Schuster

Thomas E. Dewey

Al Frueh began his career in St. Louis as a newspaper artist, and he achieved celebrity in 1907 when his caricature of the famous music-hall superkette Fritzi Scheff so offended the star that she canceled her performance. (If Frueh ever had a mean bone in his body, it must have been removed shortly thereafter.) Frueh contributed two drawings to the first issue and drew the cover for the second. In the magazine's lean early years, he produced not only caricatures but spot drawings, cartoons, and full-page sequences. The most notable of these sequences depicts a day at City Hall under the regime of the volcanic mayor Fiorello La Guardia. Frueh was not a city person and for most of his career delivered most of his work to *The New Yorker* from his nut farm in Sharon, Connecticut. Over the years *The New Yorker* added several other distinguished caricaturists to its stable, but it is Al Frueh's work that most quickly comes to mind when one thinks of *New Yorker* caricature. It was lighthearted and artful but not arty. It had the qualities Ross most admired—unpretentiousness and honesty. Frueh died in 1968 at age eighty-eight. His drawings, looked at today, seem as fresh as they did when we first published them. Even though many of his subjects are long forgotten, Al Frueh's drawings continue to charm and amuse.

Bernard M. Baruch

Murray Perahia ... André Watts ... Emanuel Ax

In the fall of 1992, I decided that after almost twenty years as art editor, it was time to cut back. Tina's magazine, it was clear, would require a whole new generation of artists, and though I still felt in touch, I believed that a younger editor might be quicker to sniff out the significant new members of that generation. I also wanted more time to do my own work. After conversations with both Bob and Tina, we agreed that I would retire as art editor at the end of 1993. In the middle of that year, Tina hired Françoise Mouly, publisher and coeditor of *Raw* magazine, to assume responsibility for the covers and non-illustrative interior color pieces. I agreed to continue on a part-time basis as cartoon editor.

When I think back over my career at *The New Yorker,* I wonder if "art editor" is the correct phrase to describe it. I tried, as any art editor should, to help the artists to bring out the best of themselves in their work. I had struggled to balance the demands of art and commerce. I'm proud of the artists I brought to the magazine, and I'm gratified by the success many of them have achieved beyond the magazine. On the other hand, the distinctive tone of the magazine's art has really been more a reflection of the editor's taste than my own. I believe this to have also been the case with Jim Geraghty and even Rea Irvin. Perhaps a more honest, if less felicitous, title for our function would be "art enablers." The credit for the art of *The New Yorker,* I'm convinced, must be divided among the artists themselves and the four ultimate editors of the magazine's art—Harold Ross, William Shawn, Robert Gottlieb, and Tina Brown.

From 1925 until 1939 the art department was actually dispersed throughout the magazine. Rea Irvin advised Ross but didn't speak to the artists. A deputy of fiction editor Katharine White spoke to the artists but had nothing to do with other aspects of art purchasing or production. The make-up department pasted up the issue but had little to do with the layout department, which laid out the front of the book—that is, "The Talk of the Town" and "Notes and Comment"—and selected the cartoons for each issue. The covers were being proofed on the business side of the magazine, and just about everyone who could hold a pencil was submitting cartoon ideas or sharpening captions.

The fiction department's dominance of the art began to wane in the late thirties, after the Whites moved to Maine. The decisive event in the evolution of the art department I inherited was the hiring of James Geraghty in 1939 to replace William Maxwell. Maxwell was the liaison to the artists and, as had his predecessors, wore two hats. He was primarily a fiction editor. Jim Geraghty was the first staff member to have no responsibilities other than the magazine's art. During the war years his position as "art editor" was officially acknowledged. Rea Irvin was declared to be "art director." When Irvin departed after Ross's death in 1951, Geraghty assumed complete responsibility for the magazine's art, and Shawn reduced the art meeting to a two-man gathering. This seemed like the natural state of affairs to me when I replaced Jim in 1973, but it's now clear that up to 1950, the art department, as I'd inherited it, had in fact not existed. Viewed from this perspective, the changes that were later made by Bob and Tina have, without conscious design, brought the magazine full circle. The art is now, as it was in the twenties, the responsibility of several hands rather than one, a situation that greatly increases the chances of discovering, as *The New Yorker* has always discovered, exciting new talent.

From 1973 to 1987 I purchased cartoons, spots, and covers, and scheduled and proofed covers, with the help of my assistant, Anne Hall, and occasionally a third person who came in one day a week to help with the filing and the returning of originals. In 1988 Bob added Chris Curry to assist with the art in the "Goings On" department. The radically expanded use of artwork under Tina Brown now requires the service of a correspondingly large team.

Illustration editor Chris Curry continues to be responsible for commissioning art for the "Goings On" section and for illustrations throughout the magazine. She meets with representatives of the "Goings On" department to select subjects for future issues every Monday. Subject to the vagaries of Tina Brown's schedule, she and Tina meet on Tuesday morning to go through finished art and discuss prospective artists. Chris now works with two assistants, and her department also includes a photography editor, Crary Pullen. Françoise Mouly is responsible for the purchase and processing of cover art and also additional interior color pieces. Françoise has added some distinctive new voices to the magazine, including the distinguished European artists Mariscal, Jacques de Loustal, and Lorenzo Mattotti. Françoise meets with Tina every Monday morning to discuss the covers and select cover pieces for future issues. The spreads themselves are designed by Caroline Mailhot and her assistant. She is also responsible for the purchase of spots and for the overall look of the magazine. Caroline meets with Tina, as the need arises, all through the week. The make-up department, now eight strong, under Pat Keogh and Mike Bullerdick, is responsible for assembling each

week's issue and transmitting it by telephone cable to our printers in Danville, Kentucky.

I continue to work with the cartoonists two days a week and meet with Tina and Rick Hertzberg at the art meeting every Tuesday afternoon to purchase cartoons. (Rick occasionally stands in for Tina when she's unavailable.) My longtime assistant, Anne Hall, now divides her time between me and Françoise Mouly. Françoise has an additional assistant, who

acts as liaison between her office and Caroline in the design department. Art Spiegelman, whom Tina hired as a contributing editor in 1993, offers in addition to his sketches and covers a steady stream of observations and suggestions. A sharp-eyed reader may have noticed how much time these editors are spending with Tina Brown. No other department, I believe, spends as much time with Tina, a fair measure of the value she places on the magazine's art. Like all the best editors, Tina is impossible to satisfy. Ross once said to Geraghty, "Good enough is not good enough," and though Tina may not be aware of that comment, it certainly is one that she would have heartily seconded. Ross and later Katharine White were notorious for pulling the magazine apart just prior to press time, and Bob and Tina seem to have the same difficult habit. Additionally, her preoccupation with timeliness, which extends from cartoons to covers, makes even long-scheduled material subject to last-minute revision. (Prior to Shawn's retirement, I scheduled covers once a month and Bob and I sometimes scheduled as much as three months ahead of time.)

This frantic pace has certainly made Tina's magazine, as she had hoped, cutting-edge, and there are no signs of her slowing down. Her taste for innovation is as keen as it was when she first started. "Talk" was revamped

for the third time in 1994, and Tina continues to experiment with new approaches to both covers and illustrations. What the final result of her restless imagination will be is impossible to predict. I am certain, however, that it will be full of energy, high spirits, and visual excitement.

Most enduring institutions rest on the solid foundation of a few simple ideas. *The New Yorker* is no exception. Ross wanted his magazine to be honest, well written, and fun to look at. He said it would be impartial and would hate bunk. Ross created, as he had hoped, a metropolitan magazine with a national audience. The magazine gained its distinct voice, lucid and skeptical, by respecting the individual voices of its contributors. It succeeded by attracting writers, editors, and artists who shared Ross's views. It still does.

ACKNOWLEDGMENTS

This book could not have been written without the cooperation and support of my colleagues at *The New Yorker*. First among them is the late James Geraghty, who brought me into the magazine as a cartoonist. I warmly thank William Shawn, who, for reasons I will never fathom, entrusted to me the care of the magazine's art after Jim's retirement, and Robert Gottlieb and Tina Brown, who asked me to continue this stewardship. In addition, both Bob and Tina have offered valuable suggestions and generously allowed me to share with the general public privileged details of the magazine's editorial life.

Ann Partrich and Chris Shay of *The New Yorker*'s library, along with Louis Rojas, Ivan Burgos, and Bruce Diones have been invaluable in their efforts to help me locate and retrieve material from the magazine's archives.

My own recollections of events have been refreshed, challenged, and occasionally revised by conversations with, among others, Roger Angell, Barbara Nicholls, Frank Modell, William Maxwell, William Fitzgerald, Albert Hubbell, Joe Carroll, Whitney Darrow, Jr., Mischa Richter, George Price, and William Steig. Former editorial counsel Joe Cooper and his assistant, Joy Weiner, have brought to my attention long-buried legal material related to the art department. The staff of the New York Public Library provided patient and tireless guidance to the recently curated *New Yorker* records now residing there. I warmly thank Rosemary Thurber for directing me to the Thurber drawings held by Ohio State University, and Geoffrey Smith of the university's Rare Books and Manuscripts Collection for guiding me through their rich file of unpublished Thurber work.

The story of James Geraghty's years as art editor could not have been written without Jim's notes for his own history of the magazine's art, and his wife Eva Geraghty graciously granted me access to these.

My assistant Anne Hall has been the right side of the art department's brain since 1973, and her recollections of our years together have clarified and amplified my own.

I acknowledge a special debt to cartoonist Robert Mankoff, who recommended to me my invaluable research assistant, Liz Haberfeld. Her creative forays into *The New Yorker* archives and beyond added much fresh and sometimes surprising material to my narrative.

The rough manuscript was shaped into publishable form, against great odds, by Rachel Peller and Kris Maher.

My agent, Martha Kaplan, has been both tactful and persuasive in steering me through midcourse corrections which led to a more comprehensive book than the one I had originally proposed.

The project could not have been completed without the enthusiastic support at Knopf of Sonny Mehta and Jane Friedman.

Knopf's copy chief Nancy Clements and the production team of Susan Chun and Jennifer Parkinson have guided me serenely through an often tangled schedule.

Peter Andersen and Arlene Lee translated my rough dummy into a volume more elegant than any I could have imagined.

The task of vetting this manuscript was handled with tact and expedition by James Buss. And the responsibility for any errors which escaped his net is, of course, mine.

Without the patience and encouragement of my editor, Katherine Hourigan, I could not have brought this sometimes leaky vessel to port.

Finally, I thank my wife, Jill, for her loving support and my daughter, Ava, for graciously allowing me to spend such a large portion of her first months on this planet with this project.

INDEX